Creative Learning Activities for Your Preschooler

Betty V. Lamb

SHADOW MOUNTAIN

Salt Lake City, Utah

To my sons, Michael, Jeremy,
Joshua, and Zachary

Shadow Mountain is an imprint of Deseret Book Company,
P.O. Box 30178, Salt Lake City, Utah 84130

First printing May 1985

Library of Congress Cataloging in Publication Data

Lamb, Betty V.
    Creative learning activities for your preschooler.

    Includes index.
    1. Domestic education. 2. Education, Preschool—
Curricula. 3. Creative activities and seat work.
I. Title.
LC37.L29   1985   649'.51   85-1620
ISBN 0-87747-924-0

Contents

Preface

Ever since I started teaching preschool over ten years ago, I have felt that the best way for a young child to learn is at home under the tutelage of his own parents. Now that I have my own children, I realize not only that this approach is better for the child, but that teaching can be a wonderful, fulfilling experience for the parents, too.

This outlook contrasts with a common belief among parents today that in order for a child to "keep up" with other children his age, he must have professional instruction before kindergarten. This belief is often denied even by professional educators. For instance, the principal of our Maryland elementary school, a man with a Ph.D. in education and many years' experience with children, believes that in the long run children who have attended formal preschools have no particular advantage over those who do not. Rather, he feels that the home environment is the most critical factor in a child's success at school—a child's best preparation for formal education is an enriched home experience.

There are many wonderful things for children to learn before they go to school, and a child's ability to learn is so high that it's a shame not to put those preschool years to good use. It is clear, however, that professional preschools are not the only way your child can receive educational training. In fact, they are only a substitute for the best teacher: *you*, teaching and loving your own preschooler at home. You know your own child—his needs, his interests, his abilities, and his weaknesses. Most importantly, if he is home with you, his early learning can be reinforced with the kind of love, understanding, and patience only you can give him. That makes *you* the professional where he is concerned.

There are many books written about child behavior, discipline, and the stages of a child's development. This book is not among them. Rather, it is written in response to many parents asking for specific ideas for teaching their own preschoolers at home. It describes activities to stimulate a child's mental, physical, and emotional growth through the use of all of his senses. The program includes a well-rounded collection of art, music, and physical exercises. Using this book, you will not simply teach facts, but you will help your child develop his natural curiosity and cultivate his imagination by expanding his experience. In all, you will help your child develop a love for learning—not necessarily to be the smartest child, but to be happy, well-adjusted, and confident. Acquiring facts will be a natural result of the development of these qualities.

Introduction

Now that you've made the commitment to teach your own child at home, you're probably wondering, "Where do I begin?" The answer is, "Right here!" We'll go step by step together. You'll find it's easier and more enjoyable than you ever dared hope it would be.

Before we get down to details, let's begin with some general pointers:

1. Keep it simple

Be aware of one potential pitfall in starting a preschool program with your child: don't make an ordeal out of it! Elaborate detailed lesson plans, strict schedules, and a classroom-like setup will only frustrate you and your child—and you'll probably give it all up, deciding it takes too much time and "Johnny isn't interested anyway."

I speak from personal experience, having read many books that outline a strict regimen for creating a child with superior mental skills. Not only can this approach be frustrating, but in my opinion it places undue pressure on a small child and can instill a fear of failure. At best, the successful child achieves a feeling of relief when a lesson is completed, not the thrill of real achievement. On the other hand, if the child has the opportunity to learn for himself, with the wise guidance of a loving parent, he can experience the thrill of achievement. He learns for his own pleasure, and not to fulfill the expectations of an adult.

The teaching format presented in this book strikes a balance between formality and spontaneity. Of course, some planning and structure will be involved—but let's make it fun!

2. Be a full-time teacher

The key to real success as a teacher is to be a *full-time* teacher. Be ready to recognize and exploit every possible teaching situation. Accurately answering your child's questions about his world is probably the best teaching opportunity you can hope for. Take advantage of it.

When your child asks you, "What happens to the sun at night?", responding that "it has gone to sleep" won't hurt him, but it will probably raise more questions than it answers. Explaining the rotation of the earth is not too advanced for a preschooler to understand. A simple demonstration with a rubber ball (earth) and a flashlight (sun) will open up exciting understanding for him, and it will take only five minutes!

My four-year-old, Michael, watching a friend fix his car, said, "I know why you have to make two holes in that can. The big one is to let the oil out, and the little one is to let the air in." Michael had asked his father only a few days before why he was putting two holes in a can. His father had taken the time to teach. Surprised at Michael's understanding, Ed responded positively, which reinforced Michael's learning.

When I was expecting Joshua, Michael, then three, had a host of questions about pregnancy. I took out a pamphlet that my obstetrician had given me that showed pictures of the developing fetus from the egg to birth. I made a story out of it, explaining the new developments of the baby each month. Michael was thrilled. For months he wanted his bedtime story to be what he called his "baby book."

As you can see, taking advantage of spontaneous learning situations can be more than an immediate response to a question. It can serve as a natural introduction to a more formal learning situation where some planning and preparation of lessons is needed. This book is designed to help you meet that need.

As you decide on a topic to teach, plan ways you can work at least part of the teaching process into your everyday activities. You will find that your conversation, your work and play, and even your meals can be geared to teaching the concepts you have chosen. You will find that this will not take a lot of extra time, and your child will respond positively to the trust you demonstrate in him as you teach him. You will also instill in him the impression that learning is a natural part of a day's activities, an attitude that will be of great value later in his life.

3. Become familiar with the whole book

The first chapter of this book consists of a series of lesson topics. The rest of the book, however, does not contain lesson plans, but consists of a variety of resource materials to help you teach the concepts in chapter 1. The lesson topics in chapter 1 are presented in no particular order, and there are many more possible topics that I have not covered. These lessons are designed for you to use according to your needs and your child's interests. Once you have used some of the lesson topics in this book, you can use them as a pattern to create lessons of your own on other topics.

Under each topic in chapter 1 is a brief introductory paragraph containing specific ideas or concepts you can teach concerning that topic. The "learning activities" that follow are the activities you may use to teach the concepts.

At the end of each lesson topic is a book list. Plan to pick up some of these books at your library before you start teaching the topic. They will provide good reviews of the concepts you're teaching, and they will ensure continuity between your lessons and your daily story time. You will also find resources for poetry, fingerplays, and songs that relate to the topic. These will enrich your lessons and provide added fun. It's important, especially for preschoolers, to incorporate such activities into the learning program.

The support material in chapters 2 through 7 provides you with tremendous flexibility in your role as teacher. Here's what these chapters contain:

Chapter 2 consists of learning games and instructions for making games, toys, and worksheets that can be used in connection with your lessons or as activities independent of your lesson topics.

Chapter 3 describes the ways your child can help with everyday meal preparation. It also contains science experiences with foods and recipes associated with the learning topics in chapter 1.

Chapter 4 contains recipes for art materials, as well as instructions and a list of supplies needed for your art projects.

Chapter 5 contains fun activities that exercise all of the parts of the body and develop coordination and balance.

Chapter 6 contains information about the best books for you to share with your preschooler.

Chapter 7 contains the instructions and patterns for specific materials needed in the individual learning topics for chapter 1.

It's time to jump in. Good luck!

Lesson Planning

The Alphabet

Learning the letters of the alphabet is important for all children before they start kindergarten. In addition to reciting the letters from memory, your child can learn how to recognize each letter by sight and that each letter has its own sound. Later, he can learn that by putting the letters together we make words.

Learning Activities:

1. Teach your child the alphabet song.

2. Teach your child to name a new letter each week. S is a good letter to start with. (Leave vowels and other letters that have more than one sound until later.) Teach all of the uppercase letters first, then the lowercase letters. (Note: In the following learning activities the letter S is used as an example.)

3. Make a capital letter S out of construction paper and put it where your child will see it often during the day (for example, on the refrigerator).

4. Teach that S says "sss." Make a game out of seeing how many words your child can name that begin with the "sss" sound.

5. Draw a large S in the middle of a paper. Have your child draw pictures of objects that begin with the "sss" sound around the big letter S.

6. Go around the house and yard and see how many things you can find that start with S.

7. Ask, "What letter says 'sss'?" (Do all of these activities each week with a different letter.)

8. Practice letter recognition and sounds with your alphabet mat (see page 75). Show your child a flash card with a letter on it; have him name the letter, find it on the mat, stand on it, and tell you what sound it makes.

9. Make your letter of the week out of sandpaper. Have your child close his eyes, feel the shape of the letter, and tell you what it is. (Guide his hand to feel the letter in the same direction the letter is formed in writing; this will help him later when he begins to write.)

10. Show your child that words are made up of letters by pointing out the "letter of the week" on cereal boxes, toys, books, signs, and so on.

11. Sing "Old MacDonald's Alphabet." Replace the animals and their sounds with letters of the alphabet and their sounds. For example: ". . . and on his farm he had a B, E-I-E-I-O. With a 'buh-buh' here . . ."

12. Play the Alphabet Chant. This is especially good for passing time in the car. Each person takes a turn with one letter of the alphabet, chanting as follows:

A, my name's Alicia
I come from Alabama
My friend's name is Aaron
And I like Apples.

The next person takes B, and the game continues through the whole alphabet. As your children get older and better at the game, you can make it harder by requiring that they' chant rhyme.

Books:

Ed Emberley's ABC, by Ed Emberley
Anno's Alphabet, by Mitsumasa Anno
A—Apple Pie, by Kate Greenaway

Songs:

Eye Winker, Tom Tinker, Chin Chopper, by Tom Glazer
  "Bingo"

Records:

Learning Basic Skills Through Music, vol. 1, by Hap Palmer
  "Marching around the Alphabet"
Ideas, Thoughts, and Feelings, by Hap Palmer
  "Letter Sounds"

Numbers

This topic is divided into two parts: (1) recognizing numerals and (2) relating numerals to numbers of items. These concepts seem closely interwoven to adults, but are really separate concepts to a child.

Part 1 Learning Activities:

1. Cut large block numbers out of sandpaper and glue them onto medium-weight cardboard. Have your child close his eyes while you guide his hand over the sandpaper numeral in the direction the numeral is formed.

2. Provide plastic numbers for free play. Magnetic numbers on a magnetic board are good learning tools.

3. Outline large block numbers on a piece of plain paper; then let your child put white glue in the numbers and fill them with beans, rice, dried corn, macaroni, glitter, and so on.

4. Play "rocket ship": Print each number from one to ten on a card. Then lay the cards on the floor in a straight row, beginning with ten. As you call out each number (ten, nine, eight . . .) your child will stand on that number until you reach one. Then he can "blast off" by jumping onto the floor.

5. Make a bingo card that contains only the numbers from one to ten. As you hold up a flash card with a number on it, your child matches it with a number on his bingo card. Have him cover the number with a poker chip or other marker (see pages 75-76).

6. Count every other number. You say "one," your child says "two," and so on.

7. Ask, "What comes after two?" "After six?" And so on. Use numbers out of sequence. If your child can't answer, go back to number one and start counting until he reaches the number you're looking for.

8. Ask, "What comes before two?" "Before six?" And so on.

9. Have your child place number flash cards in order.

10. Place several flash cards in sequence on the floor with one missing. (For example, one, two, three, and five.) Ask, "Which number is missing?"

11. Teach your child his phone number and how to call home. This is very important for safety reasons. Print your phone number on a card and have him practice calling you on a play phone. Once he has memorized the number, let him practice calling home from a pay phone or from a friend's house.

Part 2 Learning Activities:

1. Use flash cards with numbers written on them. When your child correctly identifies a number, reward him by letting him do something with it, such as clap *three* times or hop *five* times.

2. Count small groups of similar objects (such as blocks or dolls), touching each object as it is counted.

3. Sing "Ten Little Indians" using fingers to represent each Indian in the song. This is especially fun if you make little Indian finger puppets (see page 158).

4. Use dot and number cards to match numerals with groups of dots. Colored dot stickers make good cards (see page 76). You can also make additional cards with stickers of animals, flowers, and so on.

5. Count out a given number of objects from a larger number of objects. For example, have your child count three blocks out of a pile of five blocks.

6. Play "Mother, May I?" Mother says, "Take five giant steps" (or holds up a number flash card). Child responds with "Mother, may I?" before he takes the steps.

7. Hold up a flash card and have your child push to one side on an abacus the number of beads indicated by the number on the card.

8. Glue a card containing a number in the bottom of each muffin cup in a muffin tin. Use buttons, beans, colored pom-poms, or wooden beads for the child to put in each cup. (Three beads in the "3" cup, and so on.)

9. Make bingo cards with stick-ons in each square (three balloons, four cats, etc.) Have your child match numeral flash cards with the number of items on his bingo card.

10. Show your child a picture of a group of children. Ask, "How many children do you see?" "How many girls are there?" "How many have brown hair?" And so on.

11. Have your child practice writing his numbers using the "follow the dot" method (see page 86).

12. Draw groups of similar items on the left side of a paper. Write the corresponding numerals in mixed-up order on the right side of the paper. Have your child draw a line from the group of items to the numeral they represent (see page 81).

13. Once your child can write his numbers, give him papers with different numbers of objects on them (five apples, seven fish, and so on) and have him write the appropriate numeral on the paper.

14. Play the computer adding game on page 122.

Books:

Anno's Counting Book, by Mitsumasa Anno
Count and See, by Tana Hoban

Fingerplays:

Let's Do Fingerplays, by Marion F. Grayson
    "Bunnies' Bedtime"
    "Grasshoppers"
    "The Circus"

Songs:

Singing Bee! compiled by Jane Hart
    "Over in the Meadow"
    "Five Little Chickadees"
Do Your Ears Hang Low? by Tom Glazer
    "The Ants Go Marching"
    "One Finger, One Thumb"
    "Ten in a Bed"
Eye Winker, Tom Tinker, Chin Chopper, by Tom Glazer
    "Peter Hammers"
    "Ten Little Indians"
    "This Old Man"

Records:

Learning Basic Skills Through Music, vol. 1, by Hap Palmer
    "The Number March"
Learning Basic Skills Through Music, vol. 2, by Hap Palmer
    "Lucky Numbers"

Shapes

Because each shape is commonly encountered in everyday experience, practicing shape recognition is easy. Circles, squares, triangles, rectangles, stars, diamonds, ovals, and even octagons are shapes young children can learn to recognize.

Learning Activities:

1. Play a game with your child to see how many household items (such as toys) he can find that are shaped like a circle. Do the same with all of the other shapes.

2. Have a "feel box" in which you have put several items of different shapes (blocks, plastic eggs, small balls, and so on). Have your child reach in without peeking and tell you what shape he feels. After he tells you a shape, have him pull the item out so you can see if he is correct.

3. Help your child practice making shapes by tracing over dotted patterns like those used for teaching numbers and letters (see pages 85-86).

4. Let your child practice making circles on paper; then have him make a picture out of the circles. Do this with all of the shapes.

5. Relate an octagon to a stop sign. Find a picture of a stop sign in a magazine, or you can make one. Let your child color it and print the word STOP if he can. Your child will enjoy recognizing octagons as you drive. Road signs are good places to find many shapes.

6. Use masking tape to form a shape on your floor. Let your child follow the shape with his bare feet. (To make this harder, have him close his eyes.)

7. Go "fishing" for a shape. Make shapes out of colored construction paper. Place a paper clip on each shape. Put a magnet on the end of the fishing pole. Have your child name the shape as he "catches" it. You can play this game with numbers, letters, and colors, too.

Books:

The Wing on a Flea, by Ed Emberley
Circles, Triangles, and Squares, by Tana Hoban
Shapes, by John J. Reiss

Records:

Learning Basic Skills Through Music, vol. 2, by Hap Palmer
    "One Shape, Three Shapes"

Colors

Experimenting with color and the origin of color can be like magic to your child. Learning the primary colors (red, yellow, and blue) and the secondary colors (orange, green, and purple) can begin at a very young age. By age three or four your child will be able to mix his own colors for his paintings.

Learning Activities:

1. When teaching your child colors, work on one color at a time. For example, when you want to teach him red, surround him with red things all day: have him wear a red shirt, eat a red apple or red Jell-o, and play with a red ball and red blocks.

2. Play "I Spy with My Little Eye" (page 69).

3. Make a grab bag filled with colorful things. As your child pulls each item out, have him name its color.

4. Play color bingo (page 75).

5. Use clear plastic cups of water and liquid food coloring to show how secondary colors are made from primary colors. (Note: Always add a small amount of the darker color to a larger amount of the lighter color.) Practice this before you do it with your child.

6. Have available paints in the primary colors only. Tell your child you want to make a green tree. Then ask, "How can I make green?" Help him discover how to mix yellow and blue to make green. Then let him mix the other secondary colors from the primary colors and use them in his painting.

7. Help your child make a color wheel (page 83).

8. Make a rainbow by rotating a prism from a chandelier through the sunlight.

9. Tell what makes a rainbow in the sky and describe all the colors in the rainbow.

10. Make color spinners (page 165).

11. Play color relays (page 70).

12. Teach the color words by using word strips and colored chips or blocks. Have your child match the card containing the word *red* with the red block. Once he masters this skill, remove the colored blocks and have him read the words independent of any color cues.

Books:

Colors, by John J. Reiss
Little Blue and Little Yellow, by Leo Lionni
Exciting Things To Do with Color, by Janet Allen

Songs:

What Shall We Do and Allee Galloo! collected by Marie Winn
    "Jenny Jenkins"

Records:

Learning Basic Skills Through Music, vol. 1, by Hap Palmer
    "Colors"
Learning Basic Skills Through Music, vol. 2, by Hap Palmer
    "Parade Of Colors"

Telling Time

As soon as your child can recognize numerals by sight, he can begin "telling time" on a digital clock.

Learning Activities:

1. Have your child tell you what time it is several times during the day by reading the numbers on a digital clock. This is a good exercise for him in becoming acquainted with the language of time.

2. Make a clock out of a paper plate. Use the clock to begin teaching the "hour" or "o'clock." "Every time the big hand is on the 12 it is (something) o'clock." Practice with your child by moving the small hand but always leaving the big hand on 12. Once he has mastered the hour, move on to the half-hour. "Whenever the big hand is on the 6, it is (something)-thirty." Practice 4:30, 7:30, and so on.

3. The quarter hours (for example, 4:15 and 4:45) are a little harder, but with practice on a digital clock, this concept is made easier. Place a digital clock and a face clock side by side. Your child can see the placement of the hands on the face clock while reading the numerals on the digital clock.

4. Play the computer clock game on page 109.

Fingerplays:

Let's Do Fingerplays, by Marion F. Grayson
    "Clocks"

Songs:

What Shall We Do and Allee Galloo! collected by Marie Winn
    "The Clock Song"

Days of the Week

These learning activities are designed to teach your child the names of the seven days in a week.

Learning Activities:

1. The best way to teach the days of the week is by making a chart out of poster board that can be hung in your child's room. Down the left side of the chart, list the days of the week. Across from each day, place pictures of those things that symbolize the normal activities of that day. Be sure these pictures relate to the child's activities.

2. Give your child his own calendar. Mark a day that has a special event, and have your child mark off each day until the special day.

3. Hold up a finger for each day of the week as your child recites the names of the days.

4. Each morning ask your child, "What day is today?" "If today is Monday, what day was it yesterday? What day will it be tomorrow?"

Poetry:

The Moon Is Shining Bright as Day, edited by Ogden Nash
  "Days of Birth"

Months of the Year

Learning the months of the year will be a long process for your preschooler. More important than the memorization of the twelve months is helping your child get a feeling for the concepts of time and the seasons that relate to each month.

Learning Activities

1. To teach the months of the year, make a chart similar to the one described for the days of the week. Teach only four months at a time. Place pictures along the right side of the chart that symbolize important events of the month. Also use weather symbols (sun, rain, clouds) and clothing symbols according to the season of the year.

2. Teach the special holidays and family events that are related to each month. For example, your child will look forward to July if he knows that is the month of your family reunion.

3. Teach your child the month (and day) of his birthday.

Books:

A Merry-Mouse Book of Months, by Priscilla Hillman

Music

While listening to "The American Promenade," I asked four-year-old Lisa how it made her feel. She said, "Like George Washington!" Children respond to music. A happy tune will make them dance or skip. You and your child will both love playing with music, singing, and dancing together.

Learning Activities:

1. Teach rhythm through a clapping activity with your child. Start with a slow, sad rhythm. Ask, "How does that make you feel?" "What does it tell you to do?" Next try a fast and happy rhythm. Ask the same questions.

2. Play a variety of songs and clap out the rhythms with your child.

3. Have your child imitate an elephant, walking and swaying to the tune of "The Elephant Walk" from the record *Dancing Time*, by Satis N. Coleman. (Check in your local library for this record.) Or, hop like a bunny to any happy music.

4. Help your child recognize rhythms in things around him: a clock, dripping water, a metronome, the chirping of a cricket, and so on.

5. Encourage musical interest in your child by taking specific opportunities to listen to different kinds of music. Point out the music's rhythm, mood, volume, and so on. Have him pick a favorite composer or artist.

6. Children love to sing, and they love to hear you sing (even if you think you can't sing very well). Sing songs with your child.

7. Make homemade instruments. See the books listed below for instructions.

8. Show your child the different ways instruments make music by playing imaginary instruments. Blow: clarinet, trumpet, recorder, trombone. Pluck or bow: guitar, violin, cello. Strike: sticks, tambourine, drum.

9. Help your child recognize and identify the different instruments by their sounds. Two good pieces for this are "The Instruments of the Orchestra" and "Peter and the Wolf."

10. If you or another member of your family plays an instrument, let your child "play" on the instrument with your guidance.

Books:

Sounds We Hear, by Illa Podendorf
Picture Book of Musical Instruments, by Marion Lacey

Songs:

Eye Winker, Tom Tinker, Chin Chopper, by Tom Glazer
  "The Musicians"

Records:

The Feel of Music, by Hap Palmer
Movin', by Hap Palmer
Homemade Band, by Hap Palmer

All About Me

One of the greatest lessons you can teach your child is that he is important; that his ideas, his feelings, and his needs really do matter. These lessons will help him to develop a good self-image and to understand his feelings and why they change.

Learning Activities:

1. Teach your child his whole name. Ask, "What is your name?" "Jeremy." "Jeremy who?" "Jeremy David Lamb."

2. Teach your child his address and phone number.

3. Encourage individualization of interests within the members of your family by helping your child develop in the areas of his own interests and talents.

4. Reassure your child that he is capable of succeeding in tasks at home. Have him pick up his toys, set the table, make his bed, and so on.

5. Express your love for your child in different ways several times a day.

6. Encourage your child to express his emotions freely and to understand why he feels happy or sad or angry. As he verbalizes his emotions, he will learn to understand himself better.

7. Show your child pictures of children expressing different emotions. Have your child tell you what makes him feel happy, sad, angry, and so on.

8. With your child, pantomime different emotions and take turns identifying the feelings portrayed.

9. Praise your child when he is helpful and loving.

10. To help develop self-esteem, have the family gather together and play "I like you because . . ." Each member of the family takes turns telling the other members the things they like about them, or telling them something they do well. During this game, *never* say anything negative.

11. Make an "I can do" chart, and as your child learns new skills, fill in the chart. This can include tasks at home (such as making the bed) as well as mental skills (like learning the alphabet).

12. Make an "All about Me" book containing your child's own drawings. Have him begin with a self-portrait. Add pages labeled My Family, My Favorite Food, My Pet, My Home, My Best Friend, My Favorite Color, My Favorite Game, and so on. Record age, height, and weight. Include your child's handprint. Bind his book with construction-paper covers and ribbon or yarn. Let your child compare the difference in similar books each year. This book can be saved in his treasure book (see page 43).

13. Make a family tree for your child's room. Teach him that Grandma is mommy's mother, that Aunt Jeannie is mommy's sister, and so on.

14. Provide a full-length mirror in your child's room. This will help him discover himself during play.

Books:

Where the Wild Things Are, by Maurice Sendak
Alexander and the Terrible, Horrible, No Good, Very Bad Day, by Judith Viorst
Just Me, by Marie Hall Ets

Poetry:

For a Child, collected by Wilma McFarland
  "My Shadow," by Robert Louis Stevenson
Poems of Praise, selected by Pelagie Doane
  "God's Dark" (for the child who is afraid of the dark)

Fingerplays:

Let's Do Fingerplays, by Marion F. Grayson
  "Ten Fingers"
  "Mr. Thumb"
  "Right Hand, Left Hand"
  "Hands on Shoulders"
  "Who Feels Happy?"

Songs:

Do Your Ears Hang Low? by Tom Glazer
  "The Hokey Pokey"
  "I Point to Myself"
Eye Winker, Tom Tinker, Chin Chopper, by Tom Glazer
  "Where Is Thumbkin?"
What Shall We Do and Allee Galloo! collected by Marie Winn
  "Lily, Lily Wallflowers"

Records:

Learning Basic Skills Through Music, vol. 1, by Hap Palmer
  "Growing"
  "What Is Your Name?"
Getting To Know Myself, by Hap Palmer
Ideas, Thoughts and Feelings, by Hap Palmer
  "Everybody Has Feelings Like Me"

My Healthy Body

Basic nutrition, personal hygiene, and physical fitness are subjects the whole family can learn more about. Forming good health habits at a young age will benefit your child throughout his life.

Learning Activities:

1. Teach your child the four basic food groups:
   Dairy: milk, butter, cheese, ice cream
   Meat: meat, eggs, fish, poultry
   Fruits and vegetables
   Grains: bread, grains, and cereals

2. Teach your child how each of the four basic food groups helps our bodies. You can make up games to play that will help your child learn the difference between nutritious foods and junk foods. For example, show samples of different foods or pictures of food. Have your child place the foods in the categories of dairy, meat, fruits and vegetables, or grains. Explain that even though junk food won't necessarily hurt him, it won't help his body grow or become strong, so it must be eaten sparingly.

3. Let your child help you plan a meal by choosing foods he wants to eat from each of the four food groups.

4. Take your child to the grocery store and let him tell you which foods are good for him and which are not. Let him choose one healthy treat to take home.

5. Let your child help you decide how a certain food will be prepared for a meal. (For example, let him choose between cooked or raw carrots.)

6. Put several different kinds of foods (or pictures of foods) into a bag. As your child takes each item out, have him tell you whether or not it is a healthy food.

7. Provide a stool near the bathroom sink to encourage independence in personal hygiene. Encourage your child to wash his hands before eating and after using the toilet.

8. Sing "This is the way we wash our hands" to the tune of "Here We Go Round the Mulberry Bush" as you demonstrate the proper way to wash hands.

9. Plan exercises with your child that will develop muscles other than those regularly used by the child in play. Exercise together to music. Let your child explain why we need to exercise every day. (See chapter 5 for specific exercises and physical activities to do with your child.)

10. Set up an obstacle course in your backyard that includes many different skills, such as climbing over and under boxes or folding chairs, balancing while walking on a row of bricks or a string lying on the grass, skipping, hopping on one or both feet, jumping, and crawling.

11. Ask your child to show you what he can do to make his legs (arms, etc.) strong. (See specific exercises in chapter 5.)

12. After running or exercising hard, teach your child to move slowly to "cool down." He can pretend he's a rag doll moving slowly to music.

13. Give your child opportunities to get to know and trust his doctor by taking him in for a once-a-year checkup. Besides giving you the peace of mind that he is developing properly, it will build trust in your child for his doctor.

14. Go on a field trip to your local hospital. Arrange in advance with the head nurse. Hospitals often have special tours for children.

Books:

Itch, Sniffle and Sneeze, by Alvin Silverstein (about allergies)
My Doctor, by Harlow Rockwell

Poetry:

The Moon Is Shining Bright as Day, edited by Ogden Nash
    "The Germ," by Ogden Nash
Every Time I Climb a Tree, by David McCord
    "Bananas and Cream"

Learning Basic Skills: Health and Safety, by Hap Palmer
  "Take a Bath"
  "Keep the Germs Away"
  "Exercise Every Day"

Clean Teeth

After having a lesson on tooth care, four-year-old Kurt walked into the living room and found his father eating chips and drinking a soda. He said, "Daddy, that's junk food, and it's going to rot your teeth!" Practicing proper oral hygiene from an early age can reduce uncomfortable and costly dental care.

Learning Activities:

1. Most children like to brush their teeth, but they need to be encouraged to be consistent. Encourage your child to brush in the morning and at night. Supervise his brushing so that he forms good habits in his technique. Children take pride in ownership. Let your child have his own tube of toothpaste as well as his own toothbrush.

2. Cut out pictures of different kinds of foods. Prepare them for a flannel board by gluing flannel on the back of the pictures. Make a picture of a sad tooth and one of a happy tooth (see patterns on page 162). On your flannel board, have your child place the pictures of foods that are good for his teeth under the happy tooth, and the foods that are bad for his teeth under the sad tooth.

3. Take your child to the dentist to observe him working on you or another member of the family before he works on the child.

4. Your child's first visit to the dentist should be for something other than fillings (for example, a cleaning or a fluoride treatment) so that it will be a pleasant experience.

Be sure your dentist is aware that this is your child's first visit so that he can arrange to spend extra time teaching your child about dental care.

5. Ask your dentist to demonstrate to your child the proper way to brush teeth. (Most dentists keep a large toothbrush and a plastic set of teeth for this purpose.)

Books:

Our Tooth Story, by Ethel and Leonard Kessler
My Friend the Dentist, published by the Menniger Foundation
Teeth, published by Grosset and Dunlap

Records:

Learning Basic Skills: Health and Safety, by Hap Palmer
    "Brush Away"

Helping Makes Me Happy

Service brings joy. This simple concept is recognized by most adults, but it is usually hard for children to understand. Providing opportunities for your child to practice service is the best way to teach this concept.

Learning Activities:

1. Give your child a small job around the house that he can successfully complete. (Setting the table, making his bed, sweeping the floor, or picking up his toys.) Give very simple instructions on how the job is done. Then let him do it. After he is finished, praise him for a job well done. Let him know how much it really does help you when he does his jobs. Encourage him to express his happy feelings for being

big enough to help. (Don't redo the job you have asked your child to do. If the job must be improved on, take him with you and redo it together explaining how to do it correctly.)

2. Plan a family activity to help someone else, such as going to a rest home to read or sing to those who live there or helping a widowed neighbor by pulling the weeds in her garden.

3. Let your child choose a food he wants to help you prepare for dinner. Let him do every step he possibly can. Praise his accomplishment while you're eating.

4. Have your child commit to be a special helper to a younger brother or sister for a day. Let him decide what specific things he will do to help.

Books:

Billy and Our New Baby, by Helene S. Arnstein
Stone Soup, by Marcia Brown
Pelle's New Suit, by Elsa Beskow
A Treeful of Pigs, by Arnold Lobel

Poetry:

A Small Child's Book of Verse, compiled by Pelagie Doane
    "Kindness to Animals"

Fingerplays:

Let's Do Fingerplays, by Marion F. Grayson
    "Helpfulness"

Songs:

Singing Bee! compiled by Jane Hart
    "Little Drops of Water"
Eye Winker, Tom Tinker, Chin Chopper, by Tom Glazer
    "The More We Are Together"
    "The Mulberry Bush"

Smell

Learning Activities:

1. Put the following items into small jars (such as baby-food jars) and let your child guess what the items are by the smell: perfume, vanilla, cinnamon, orange peel, onions.

2. Mealtime is a natural time to talk about the smells of food. Use foods with distinctive odors during this lesson: bacon, broccoli, spaghetti sauce, peanut butter, or cinnamon toast.

3. Have your child plug his nose and taste a small piece of a raw potato and a small piece of apple (both peeled). See if he can tell the difference without smelling them.

4. Have your child close his eyes. Let him smell a piece of apple, but put a small piece of raw potato into his mouth to eat. Ask, "What are you eating?"

5. Play an imaginary smelling game. Have your child pretend he is walking through the woods. Ask him to describe what he smells. (Use any environment that your child is familiar with: the beach, a lake, the zoo.)

6. During bathtime, talk about the clean smell of soap.

Poetry:

A Small Child's Book of Verse, compiled by Pelagie Doane
  "Smells," by Christopher Morley

Sight

Learning Activities:

1. Ask your child to show you all the things he can do with his eyes (see, blink, open, close, wink, roll).

2. Place five small objects on the floor and talk about each one. (Use things the child is familiar with: clothespin,

ball, block, toy car, doll, puzzle piece, plastic farm animal, pencil.) Have him look carefully at all of the objects and then close his eyes. Take one object away and then have him tell you what is missing. As he gets better at this game, put in more objects, or use colored blocks and have him tell you what color is missing.

3. Play "I Spy with My Little Eye." You say, "I spy with my little eye something that is red." Your child guesses everything he sees that is red until he guesses the object you had in mind. Take turns being the spy.

4. Obtain objects that can be distinguished only by sight (such as crayons or colored blocks). Have your child close his eyes and see if he can tell you the difference between the objects.

5. Look through a magnifying glass at common household items. How do they look different than with just your eyes?

6. Have your child look into a mirror and observe the size of his pupil. Have him close his eyes for thirty seconds and then look again. How did the pupil change? Why?

Books:

Look! How Your Eyes See, by Marcel Sislowitz

Touch

Learning Activities:

1. Make a "feel box" by putting small objects in an empty box. Have your child tell what each object is just by feeling it. You can include bottle caps, clothespins, pencils, scissors, blocks, spoons, small toys, comb, brush, and so on.

2. Make two feel boxes (or bags) with identical items in each one. Have your child find pairs by touch and pull them out of the boxes.

3. Use a heating pad and an ice pack to demonstrate hot and cold.

4. Check with your library for the Disney filmstrip *Our Sense of Touch.*

5. Make a "feel" collage using pieces of sandpaper, cotton balls, salt, rice, beans, and so on (see page 140).

6. Play "Simon Says" (page 68).

7. At mealtime talk about the texture of foods: crunchy carrots, sticky peanut butter, smooth ice cream, and so on.

8. Mention different objects and have your child indicate whether they are hot, warm, cool, or cold: bathwater, a glass of milk, ice cubes, a campfire.

9. Make a touch book (page 168).

Books:

Pat the Bunny, by Dorothy Kunhardt
Touch Will Tell, by Marcia Brown

Poetry:

A Small Child's Book of Verse, compiled by Pelagie Doane
    "Mud," by Polly Chase Boyden

Taste

Learning Activities:

1. At dinner, have your child express how foods taste with words like "salty" or "sweet" rather than "good" or "bad."

2. Place in small jars the following: salt, sugar, flour, powdered sugar, lemon juice, and molasses. One by one, put a bit of each one on your child's tongue and have him describe the taste.

3. Explore the different tastes of foods in the raw state as compared to when they are cooked (carrots, broccoli, cauliflower, apples, mushrooms).

Hearing

Learning Activities:

1. Sit with your child. When everything is very quiet, have him tell you what he hears. (The motor of the refrigerator, a dripping faucet, a car driving by, an airplane overhead.)

2. Tape-record several different sounds, or find a sound-effects record at the library. Have your child identify the sounds.

3. Use several toys that make sounds. Have your child close his eyes and guess what each toy is by the sound it makes.

4. Fill pop bottles with different levels of water. Blow in the bottles or tap them with a spoon. Talk about the difference in sounds because of the different levels of the water.

5. Check with your library for a record of animal sounds. Have your child name each animal by the sound it makes.

6. Play "Hop and Stop." Have your child hop up and down or stop as you beat a drum. One beat means go, and two fast beats mean stop. If the child forgets to listen, he has to start over.

7. Listen to a seashell.

8. Play "Name That Tune" using the piano or humming slowly until your child guesses what the song is.

Books:

My Five Senses, by Aliki
The Seashore Noisy Book, by Margaret Wise Brown
I Went for a Walk, by Lois Lenski

Poetry:

A Small Child's Book of Verse, compiled by Pelagie Doane
    "Extremes," by James Whitcomb Riley
For a Child, collected by Wilma McFarland
    "Kitchen Tunes," by Ida M. Pardue

Fall

In the autumn, leaves on the trees turn gold, orange, and red and fall to the ground. Many animals store nuts and other foods to use during the cold winter months to follow. Foods ripen and are ready to be harvested. The cool days and crisp nights bring an end to the hot summer.

Learning Activities:

1. Use a weather chart (page 64) to show that fall comes after summer.

2. Take out your child's fall clothing and launder them with your child. Talk about the difference between these clothes and the ones he's been wearing all summer.

3. Go on a nature walk with your child and have him gather leaves and anything else related to fall. Make a collage out of the things you've gathered.

4. Go for a drive through a canyon or forest to observe the changing color in the leaves.

5. Make leaf rubbings (page 142).

6. Rake a pile of leaves with your child and run and jump in them.

7. Observe with your child the migration of birds.

8. Take your child to a park to observe squirrels storing nuts for the winter.

9. Involve your child in your harvest projects; harvesting the garden, canning fruits and vegetables, and so on.

Books:

Johnny Maple-Leaf, by Alvin Tresselt
The True Book of Seasons, by Illa Podendorf

Poetry:

Every Time I Climb a Tree, by David McCord
   "The Wind"
For a Child, collected by Wilma McFarland
   "Come, Little Leaves," by George Cooper

Fingerplays:

Let's Do Fingerplays, by Marion F. Grayson
   "Whirling Leaves"
   "Apples"
   "Five Little Squirrels"

Winter

In the winter the weather turns very cold, and in many parts of the country it snows. Children love to have Mom and Dad join in their winter fun: playing in the snow, building snowmen, skating, and having snowball fights. Heavy clothing, coats, hats, and mittens help to keep us warm in the cold and the snow.

Learning Activities:

1. Put water in paper cups and set them outside overnight. Explain to your child how and why the water changed to ice.

2. Take out some of your child's summer clothes and some of his winter clothes. Have him explain what type of weather each would be worn in, and why.

3. Bring in a tub of snow and let your child play in it with measuring spoons, cups, wooden spoons, and so on.

4. Take your child outside and make angels in the snow.

5. Make snow cones by gathering clean snow in a paper cup and sprinkling the top with Jell-o powder. Use only freshly fallen, deep snow.

6. Pantomime building a snowman. Your child will follow your lead as you roll the balls and place one on top of the other. Add a hat, scarf, eyes, nose, and mouth.

7. Wet dark-blue construction paper with a sponge and "paint" it with white chalk to make a snowstorm.

8. Make up a snow story with your child. Take turns adding each new event to the story.

9. Make a thermometer (page 63).

Books:

The Snowy Day, by Ezra Jack Keats
White Snow, Bright Snow, by Alvin Tresselt
The Mitten, by Alvin Tresselt

Poetry:

The First Book of Poetry, selected by Isabel J. Peterson
    "Falling Snow"
    "The Snowman's Resolution," by Aileen Fisher
"The New Nutcracker Suite and Other Innocent Verses, by Ogden Nash
    "Winter Morning"

A Small Child's Book of Verse, compiled by Pelagie Doane
    "Icy," by Rhoda W. Bacmeister
    "Jack Frost," by Helen Bayley Davis
    "The Little Red Sled," by Jocelyn Bush
Every Time I Climb a Tree, by David McCord
    "Snowman"
    "The Frost Pane"
    "Joe"
For a Child, collected by Wilma McFarland
    "A Sledding Song," by Norman C. Schlichter
    "Winter Night," by Mary F. Butts
    "A Popcorn Song," by Nancy Byrd Turner

Fingerplays:

Let's Do Fingerplays, by Marion F. Grayson
    "The Mitten Song"
    "Big Hill"
    "Snowflakes"

Spring

Nature displays many changes in the spring. The snow melts as the days get warmer. Baby animals are born, the grass turns green, flowers begin to bloom, and gardens are planted.

Learning Activities:

1. Go on a "discover spring" excursion in a park or other outdoor recreation area where trees and flowers are growing. Look carefully under stones and in the grass for new sprouts. Use a magnifying glass.

2. Make a popcorn tree (the popcorn looks like spring blossoms) by gluing popcorn onto the bare branches of a tree made out of construction paper. When popping the

corn, lay out a clean sheet on the floor and place the corn popper in the center with the lid off. Stand back and watch the corn fly as it pops! (Be careful of hot unpopped kernels.)

3. Read *The Carrot Seed*, by Ruth Krauss. This is a good story for children to act out.

4. Help your child plant a bean seed in a clear plastic cup. Teach him how to care for it so it will grow. As the seed sprouts, he will be able to see the roots through the cup. (Be sure to use fresh seeds that will sprout.)

5. Pantomime to the tune of "The Mulberry Bush." Sing, "This is the way we plant the seed (water the seed, pull the weeds, and so on)."

6. Let your child help you plant your garden and care for your yard. Perhaps he could have his own section of the garden to plant and care for by himself. If you don't have a garden, you could use a planter.

7. At your library, check out the "Life Cycle of a Frog" sequence charts by Child's World.

8. Visit a fish or chicken hatchery. Call ahead to find out when it would be most convenient to see the babies hatching.

9. If the opportunity arises, allow your child to witness the live birth of an animal.

10. Make a life-cycle-of-a-butterfly chart (page 156).

11. Make a butterfly that really flies (page 11).

Books:

Spring Is Here, by Lois Lenski
My Puppy Is Born, by Joanna Cole
Kid's Gardening, by Aileen Paul

Poetry:

For a Child, collected by Wilma McFarland
    "March," by Sara Henderson Hay
    "Rain," by Robert Louis Stevenson

"The Romp," by Nancy Byrd Turner
"Baby Seed Song," by Evelyn Nesbit
"Who Has Seen the Wind?" by Christina G. Rossetti
A Small Child's Book of Verse, compiled by Pelagie Doane
"I Heard It in the Valley," by Annette Wynne
"Wise Johnny," by Edwina Fallis
"Spring," by Laura E. Richards
"How the Flowers Grow," by Gabriel Setoren
Every Time I Climb a Tree, by David McCord
"Cocoon"

Fingerplays:

Let's Do Fingerplays, by Marion F. Grayson
"My Garden"

Songs:

Singing Bee! compiled by Jane Hart
"The Caterpillar"
"Oats, Peas, Beans"
Do Your Ears Hang Low? by Tom Glazer
"Can You Plant a Cabbage?"

Summer

Summer is a time for family fun: swimming, camping, and playing outdoors. Lightweight clothing helps keep us cool during the long, hot days.

Learning Activities:

1. Use a weather chart to show that summer comes after spring (page 64).

2. Using an outdoor thermometer or the weather forecast from the television or radio, find out the day's

temperature. Help your child move the "mercury" on his play thermometer (page 63) to the day's forecast. Let him tell you what kind of clothing would be appropriate for the day.

3. Make your summer vacation plans together as a family. Let your children help you choose some of the activities they want to do during the vacation.

4. Unpack your family's summer clothing and talk about why we wear lightweight clothing in the summer.

5. Go on a walk and see how many signs of summer you can discover: flowers blooming, children out of school, people in lightweight clothing, people working in their yards and gardens, and so on.

6. Make homemade ice cream as a family.

Books:

On a Summer Day, by Lois Lenski
The Fourth of July Story, by Alice Dalgliesh
Rain, by Peter Spier

Poetry:

For a Child, collected by Wilma McFarland
    "The Little Turtle," by Vachal Lindsay
    "The Swing," by Robert Louis Stevenson
    "The Rainbow," by Christina G. Rossetti
A Small Child's Book of Verse, compiled by Pelagie Doane
    "Swimming," by Clinton Scollard
    "Mud Cakes," by Mildred D. Shacklett
Every Time I Climb a Tree, by David McCord
    "The Pickety Fence"

Fingerplays:

Let's Do Fingerplays, by Marion F. Grayson
    "Two Little Ducks"

Halloween

Halloween can be a time of fear and apprehension for preschoolers. It is wise for parents to play down the scary parts of Halloween and concentrate on fun. Wearing hats and painting faces is better for this age than wearing masks and "being" goblins or skeletons. Halloween is a time for make-believe, and children love to pretend. Second only to Christmas, Halloween is *the* holiday of the year for children. Because Halloween comes during harvest time, pumpkins, apples, and popcorn are used as part of the celebration.

Learning Activities:

1. If you don't have your own garden, take your child to a farm to show him how pumpkins and other foods grow. Let him choose his own pumpkin to take home.

2. Let your child help you carve a jack-o-lantern out of his pumpkin. Save the seeds. They can be planted in the spring, or cleaned and toasted (page 129) as part of your Halloween celebration, or they can be dyed to make a Halloween collage (page 140).

3. Make Halloween cookies, popcorn balls, or doughnuts.

4. Use a fresh pumpkin to make pumpkin pie, pumpkin cake, or pumpkin bread. Let your child participate from beginning to end so he can make the connection between the pumpkin and the pie.

5. Make cheese jack-o-lanterns by using a jack-o-lantern cookie cutter on pre-sliced cheese. This makes a fun snack during the Halloween season.

6. Let your child choose what he wants to be for Halloween, with your limitations (for example, ask your child, "Would you rather be a clown or a tiger?")

7. Make small batches of red and yellow playdough. Let your child knead them together to make orange. (Recipe on page 136.)

8. Let your child create his own trick-or-treat bag by cutting out and gluing on Halloween shapes, or by drawing them on.

9. Make "ghost" lollipops (page 134).

Books:

That Terrible Halloween Night, by James Stevenson
Trick or Treat, by Louis Slobodkin
From Seed to Jack-o-Lantern, by Hannah Lyons Johnson

Poetry:

A Small Child's Book of Verse, compiled by Pelagie Doane
 "Hallowe'en," by Anna Medary
 "Black and Gold," by Nancy Byrd Turner
Every Time I Climb a Tree, by David McCord
 "The Witch"

Fingerplays:

Let's Do Fingerplays, by Marion F. Grayson
 "Halloween Witches"
 "Jack-O'-Lanterns"

Songs:

Eye Winker, Tom Tinker, Chin Chopper, by Tom Glazer
 "Jack-O'-Lantern"

Thanksgiving

The Pilgrims and Indians celebrated the first Thanksgiving party at Plymouth. Thanksgiving is the celebration of the harvest and a time to recognize and express thankfulness. We gather together as families on Thanksgiving to express our love for each other and our gratitude for our families, friends, homes, and food.

Learning Activities:

1. Teach your child the following story of the first Thanksgiving, using a flannel board or hand-held pictures. Also, use a world globe to show how far the Pilgrims traveled.

Over three hundred years ago some people who lived in England were not happy because the king of England said they all had to go to his church. They heard about a land far across the ocean called America. They decided to come to America so they could be free and go to the church they liked.

A big ship called the *Mayflower* took these people, who are called the Pilgrims, to America. The trip was very long. They landed in America in November, and it was very cold. They called their new town Plymouth.

The pilgrims cut down trees to make their houses, tables, chairs, and beds.

The Indians were friendly and helpful. They taught the Pilgrims how to plant corn, pumpkins, and other foods, and how to hunt. The Indians taught the pilgrim children how to pop popcorn.

In the fall there was a big harvest. The Pilgrims put away food for the long winter.

The Pilgrims were very happy. They went to church and thanked God for their good harvest. After church they had a big feast, the first Thanksgiving dinner. They

invited the Indians to join them for their big dinner. The
Pilgrims and the Indians ate together and played games.
The celebration lasted for three days.

2. Make or buy a small cornucopia. For several weeks
before Thanksgiving, have your children write on slips of
paper what they are thankful for and put the papers in the
cornucopia. (Young children can have older brothers and
sisters or parents help with the writing.) After your Thanksgiving dinner, when you are all together, read the papers.

3. Make a picture of the *Mayflower* (page 167).

4. Make Indian necklaces. Paint large macaroni with
food coloring. Let the macaroni dry. String it on colored
yarn.

5. Make apple turkeys as place markers for your dinner
table (page 129).

6. Make "Punkin Puddin' " (page 129).

Books:

Little Bear's Thanksgiving, by Janice
The Thanksgiving Story, by Alice Dalgliesh
The Popcorn Book, by Tomie de Paola

Poetry:

For a Child, collected by Wilma McFarland
    "First Thanksgiving of All," by Nancy Byrd Turner

Fingerplays:

Let's Do Fingerplays, by Marion F. Grayson
    "Our Table"

Songs:

Singing Bee! compiled by Jane Hart
    "Over the River"

Christmas

Christmas is a time for fun with our families; making cookies and gifts, decorating the tree and the house, and singing Christmas carols. As we teach our children the arts of giving and service, we learn to understand the love Christ taught and the purpose for his birth.

Learning Activities:

1. Read the account of Christ's birth from the New Testament (Luke 2:1-14).

2. Act out the story of the first Christmas.

3. Help your child make gifts for each member of your family. Also let him decorate paper and use it to wrap the gifts. Vegetable printing (page 141) is a good way to make wrapping paper.

4. String popcorn and cranberries for the tree.

5. Make paper chains for the tree (page 160).

6. In addition to the more popular Christmas songs, expose your child to greater pieces like those from Handel's *Messiah*.

7. Teach your child to give by incorporating into your Christmas traditions such activities as taking plates of cookies to neighbors, giving a Christmas surprise anonymously to a needy family, or going to nursing homes or children's wards in hospitals to sing carols.

8. Make a sweet-roll Christmas tree (page 127).

9. Make graham-cracker gingerbread houses (page 133).

Books:

The Clown of God, by Tomie de Paola
The Friendly Beasts, illustrated by Tomie de Paola
Christmas, by Peter Spier
Morris's Disappearing Bag, by Rosemary Wells
    There are many Christmas craft books to choose from.
Look in your library.

Poetry:

The New Nutcracker Suite and Other Innocent Verses, by
Ogden Nash
    "The New Nutcracker Suite"
For a Child, collected by Wilma McFarland
    "Christmas Coming!" by Dorothy Brown Thompson
    "Christmas for Me," by J. Lilian Vandevere
A Small Child's Book of Verse, compiled by Pelagie Doane
    "Long, Long Ago"
Every Time I Climb a Tree, by David McCord
    "Come Christmas"

Fingerplays:

Let's Do Fingerplays, by Marion F. Grayson
    "Christmas Is Coming"

Songs:

Singing Bee! compiled by Jane Hart
    "Pat-a-Pan"
    "Jingle Bells"

Valentine's Day

    Valentine's Day is a special day to show our family and
friends that we love them.

Learning Activities:

1. Encourage your child to talk about Valentine's Day; why we have it, what we do on it, and how we can express our love for our families and friends.

2. Together with your child, make Valentine cookies to share with his friends.

3. Provide the materials your child will need to make Valentines for grandparents and friends (colored paper, doilies, glitter, lace).

4. Make valentine decorations for your dinner table.

Books:

Hearts, Cupids and Red Roses, by Edna Barth (an adult reference book)

Poetry:

A Small Child's Book of Verse, compiled by Pelagie Doane
   "A Valentine," by Eleanor Hammond

Saint Patrick's Day

Saint Patrick is remembered because it is believed that he rid Ireland of all serpents. Symbols of Saint Patrick's Day are shamrocks, Leprechauns, and the color green. It is a day for make-believe and fun.

Learning Activities:

1. Using a flannel board, present the story of Saint Patrick and how he rid Ireland of its serpents.

2. Make shamrocks to decorate your house and dinner table (page 161).

3. Cut shamrocks out of heavy paper or lightweight cardboard and do crayon rubbings (page 142).

4. Whisper the following story about Leprechauns (pictures of Leprechauns are available through greeting-card stores):

> Leprechauns are little make-believe shoemakers who live in Ireland. (Show your child where Ireland is on a globe or a map.) On Saint Patrick's Day, if you listen very carefully, you can hear the tap-tap-tapping of their little hammers as they make shoes. If you can catch a Leprechaun, they have to give you a pot of gold! But watch out! They are very tricky.

Follow up by emphasizing that Leprechaun's are make-believe. "Are there really Leprechauns? No, but we can pretend for fun."

5. Do the Dance of the Leprechauns (the Irish Jig) with your child.

6. Make shamrock cookies to share with friends (color the batter green!).

7. What happens if you don't wear green on Saint Patrick's day? (You get pinched.)

8. Go on a shamrock hunt in a clover field—pretend the four-leaf clovers are shamrocks.

9. To *really* get into the spirit of Saint Patrick's Day, use food coloring to color your scrambled eggs, butter for your toast, or pancake batter for breakfast. At dinner, be sure to serve green vegetables and green Jell-o. Add green food coloring to your dinner roll dough. Drink lime-ade.

10. Make Marilyn's Leprechaun Soup (page 128).

Books:

Shamrocks, Harps and Shillelaghs, by Edna Barth (an adult reference book)

Easter

Easter is the celebration of life. It comes in the spring when everything is new. The grass is green, flowers begin to bloom, and baby animals are born. Easter eggs and blossoming flowers remind us of the new life Jesus gave us. Easter Sunday is a special, joyful day, a day to remember Jesus.

Learning Activities:

1. Retell the story of the resurrection of Christ as found in the New Testament in John chapter 20 (use pictures as you tell the story).

2. Attend Easter services in your church with your family.

3. Color Easter eggs together.

4. Go on an Easter-egg hunt.

5. Make flowers for home decorations.

6. If you make or buy new clothes for Easter, explain their symbolism. (Just as the earth puts on its new clothes of greenery, we dress in new clothes for Easter.)

7. Get an incubator and hatch baby chicks. (Do this far enough in advance so the eggs will hatch on or around Easter.)

8. Make Jell-o eggs (page 132).

Books:

Humbug Rabbit, by Lorna Balian

Songs:

Singing Bee! compiled by Jane Hart
   "The Easter Bunny"

May Day

The first day of May is called May Day. On May Day, we make paper baskets and fill them with popcorn and candy or flowers and give them to our friends. This is a special day for us to show our friends that we love them. The celebration of May Day is believed to have originated from the Russian Festival of Flowers.

Learning Activities:

1. Make May baskets with your child. There is a pattern on page 163, or you can use margarine tubs, berry baskets, or any other small container on which you could attach handles made from colored pipe cleaners or construction paper. Decorate the baskets with paper flowers or drawings.

2. Make popcorn.

3. Fill each basket with popcorn, corn candy, and new spring violets.

4. Have your child hang the basket on the doorknob of a friend's house, ring the bell, and run and hide until the basket is discovered.

5. Use a pole on a swing-set as a maypole. Tape crepe-paper streamers to the top of the pole. Have each child hold the end of a streamer. Every other child will go to the left; the others will go to the right. The children remain dancing in the same direction but weave the streamers over and then under the children they are passing as they dance.

Birthdays

Your birthday is the celebration of the day you were born. Each birthday adds one year to your age.

Learning Activities:

1. Show your child pictures of himself as a newborn baby. Explain that his birthday is the celebration of the day he was born.

2. Show your child pictures of himself on his other birthdays and explain how on each birthday he adds one year to his age.

3. Ask "If you are three years old today, how old will you be on your next birthday?"

4. Help your child make gifts or cards for brothers', sisters', and grandparents' birthdays.

5. Help your child to know how special he is to you by making his birthday a big day for the whole family.

6. Create special family traditions related to birthdays, such as a night out alone with Mom and Dad, friends over for a slumber party, a surprise hidden under his overturned dinner plate, or no work for a whole day!

7. Help your child memorize his birth date. Teach him how he can tell when it is getting close. ("When spring is here, then your birthday will come.")

8. On each of your child's birthdays, write him a letter telling him the big events of the year, the cute things he said and did, the new things he learned, and, most importantly, how much you love him and how glad you are he's part of your family. Put the letters in a book or save them in a safe place until he is old enough to read them.

9. Make a "treasure book" for your child. On each birthday bring this scrapbook of pictures up to date. Also, write in it about "firsts," such as the first time your child writes his name or has his hair cut. Include any ribbons, certificates, or awards he receives.

10. Make a birthday crown (page 164).

Books:

The Birthday Tree, by Ethel Collier
A Birthday Wish, by Ed Emberley

Poetry:

The New Nutcracker Suite and Other Innocent Verses, by Ogden Nash
   "Between Birthdays"
A Small Child's Book of Verse, compiled by Pelagie Doane
   "Little Brother's Secret," by Katherine Mansfield

Policemen

Many children are afraid of policemen, probably because of their image portrayed on television. It is important that children understand that policemen are the "good guys" and do more than chase criminals. They help lost children find their homes, they make sure people are driving safely, they direct traffic, and they can give first aid if someone is hurt. If you need help, you can call on a policeman and he will help you.

Learning Activities:

1. If you have a policeman in your neighborhood, ask him if he will show your child his car (or motorcycle), radio, badge, and so on, and explain to your child all of the different jobs he does.

2. Call your local police department and arrange for a time when you and your child can go to the department and observe what policemen do.

3. Ask the police chief (or officer) to stress to your child the importance of children not talking to strangers or *ever*

getting into anyone's car unless his parents are present. Follow up by teaching your child what he should do if a stranger ever approaches him.

4. Teach your child how to use the emergency phone number 911. Practice dialing with the receiver button depressed. Emphasize how important it is not to "cry wolf" by using this number improperly.

5. Role-play "policeman" with your child to help him understand how a policeman could help him if he is lost or needs help.

Books:

Our Friend the Policeman, by David Cuniff
Policeman Small, by Lois Lenski

Fire Safety and Firemen

The following concepts of fire safety are very important for your child to understand.

1. Fire is hot.
2. Things that are hot can burn you.
3. You must never play with matches.
4. Firemen help us by fighting fires.
5. Firemen have special clothes they must wear while they are fighting fires.
6. Cool water helps a burn stop hurting.
7. If your clothes catch fire, drop to the floor and roll over and over to put out the flames. (This may be frightening to children, but it is very important that they practice this so that if it ever does happen, they will know what to do and will not try to run away from it. Reassure your child that this is a rare possibility but that you want him to be prepared.)

8. If you are in a building that is on fire, crawl on your hands and knees under the smoke to get out.

9. If you find a fire, call "Fire!" to attract the attention of a grown-up. (Caution your child on the danger of "crying wolf".)

Learning Activities:

1. Using your water faucets, teach your child that "H" means "hot" and "C" means "cold."

2. Point out all of the things in the house that are potentially hot: stove, lightbulbs, hot water, fireplace, and so on.

3. Teach your child to always tell you if he finds matches. Show him why he must never play with matches.

4. Plan and practice a fire escape drill from all of the rooms in your home. Practice crawling on hands and knees as if the room were filled with smoke.

5. Practice dropping to the floor and rolling to put out burning clothing. (Never run away!)

6. If your child gets a minor burn, put the burned area in cool water. Major burns should also be placed in cool water but will need the attention of a doctor as well.

7. Take a trip to your local fire station. Plan this in advance with the firemen. Ask them to show your child the equipment and clothing used by the firemen when they are at a fire. If a small child is in a fire and has never seen a fireman in his fire-fighting suit, a fireman may be frightening to him. For this reason it is good for the child to see the fireman put his clothing on during his visit to the fire station.

Books:

The Little Fire Engine, by Lois Lenski
The Little Fireman, by Margaret Wise Brown

Fingerplays:

Let's Do Fingerplays, by Marion F. Grayson
   "Ten Little Firemen"

Street Safety

Street signs can warn your child of danger even if he can't read yet. The signs warn by their color and shape. Red means stop; yellow means be careful; green means go. It is important to obey traffic signs for our own safety and for the safety of others.

Learning Activities:

1. Packets of traffic symbols can be purchased at educational supply stores, or you can make your own from construction paper. Common signs that children should be aware of are Stop, Yield, School, Pedestrian Crossing, and Bicycle Paths. Show the traffic signs and explain what they mean and how they can help keep us safe.

2. Using the signs, ask your child where each would be found and what would happen if we did not obey the sign.

3. Using the signs, teach your child that the colors on the signs always mean the same thing; for example, a Yield sign is yellow. It means "Stop . . . look . . . proceed." A Do Not Enter sign is red and means "Stop and go another way." School signs and crosswalk signs are yellow. They mean "Be careful; watch for children and people who are walking." A Bike Path sign is green. It means "This is where you go when you're riding a bike." Blue signs give directions to services. For example, a phone sign or a hospital sign is blue.

4. Point out traffic signs as you drive or walk along the street. Remind your child of the importance of observing traffic signs.

5. Make a street light out of a quart-sized milk carton. Cover the carton with white paper. Glue on red, yellow, and green construction-paper "lights" in the proper places.

6. Play "Red Light, Green Light" (page 70).

7. Role play with your child what happens if you disobey the traffic signs. You could use toy cars and people, or you could have one child be a pedestrian and another child be a car.

Books:

Green Says Go, by Ed Emberley

Fingerplays:

Let's Do Fingerplays, by Marion F. Grayson
    "Driving Down the Street"

Records:

Learning Basic Skills: Health and Safety, by Hap Palmer
    "Safeway"
    "Stop, Look and Listen"

Land Transportation

Cars, buses, trucks, and trains carry people and cargo across the land. Cars have safety belts and door locks to help keep us safely inside. Many large trucks carry food and clothing to the stores so we can buy these things.

Learning Activities:

1. See how many vehicles your child can name for traveling on land. Draw simple pictures of each, pointing out the differences.

2. As you travel, ask your child to tell what he thinks could be in the trucks and trains you pass.

3. Explain why it is helpful to us to have trucks and trains that can carry cargo from one place to another.

4. Help your child to be safety conscious by assigning him to see that everyone locks their car doors when you travel and by letting him remind everyone to buckle their seat belts.

5. Take your child on a train ride. Arrange with the conductor to let him go into the caboose and the engine.

6. Explain the different kinds of cars on a train and what they are used for.

Books:

The Train, by David McPhail
Truck, by Donald Crews
The Little Engine That Could, by Watty Piper

Poetry:

The First Book of Poetry, selected by Isabel J. Peterson
    "From a Railway Carriage," by Robert Louis Stevenson
For a Child, collected by Wilma McFarland
    "Travel," by Edna St. Vincent Millay

Fingerplays:

Let's Do Fingerplays, by Marion F. Grayson
    "Choo Choo Train"

Songs:

Singing Bee! compiled by Jane Hart
    "Down by the Station"
    "Working on the Railroad"
Eye Winker, Tom Tinker, Chin Chopper, by Tom Glazer
    "The Bus Song"

What Shall We Do and Allee Galloo! collected by Marie Winn
   "Chug-a-Lug-a-Lug (Train a Comin')"

Records:

Learning Basic Skills: Health and Safety, by Hap Palmer
   "Buckle Your Seatbelt"

Water Transportation

A boat is made to float on the water. People can travel across the water in a boat. They can be made to move through the water by wind blowing in the sails, rowing with oars, or by motors.

Learning Activities:

1. Will it float or will it sink? Have your child play with several different objects while he is in the bathtub. Ask him to guess if an object will float or sink before he tries it. Try some of the following items: nail, rock, wood chips, cork, styrofoam, spools, cups, soap.

2. Use a balloon in the tub to demonstrate how air makes things float.

3. Explain that once someone learns how to swim and breathe properly while swimming, the air in his lungs helps him to float just like the air in the balloon.

4. Show pictures of different kinds of boats. Have your child describe what each kind of boat is used for.

5. Play "Row, Row, Row Your Boat" (page 146).

6. Play "Motor Boat" (page 146).

7. Demonstrate how a submarine works. Place a small empty glass jar with the lid on into a tub of water. Then take the lid off and allow the water to seep in so that the "submarine" will go underwater.

Books:

The Travels of J.B. Rabbit, by Doris Susan Smith

Poetry:

For a Child, collected by Wilma McFarland
    "Where Go the Boats?" by Robert Louis Stevenson
    "Ferryboats," by James S. Tippett
    "I Saw a Ship a-Sailing," Old Nursery Rhyme

Songs:

Singing Bee! compiled by Jane Hart
    "Row, Row, Row Your Boat"
    "Lightly Row"
What Shall We Do and Allee Galloo! collected by Marie Winn
    "A Big Ship Sailing"

Air Transportation

Airplanes carry people, letters, and packages from one place to another by flying in the air. Airplanes use propellers, wings, and an engine to get up into the air. Jets, missiles, helicopters, and piper cubs are different kinds of airplanes.

Learning Activities:

1. Take a trip to the airport to observe all that happens there. Point out how to buy a ticket, check luggage, and board the plane. Show how the luggage and food trucks work to load the plane. Notice all the different jobs people have at an airport.

2. Show pictures of different kinds of aircraft. Point out the parts: wings, propeller, cockpit, engines.

3. Go on an imaginary plane ride. Buy a ticket, board the airplane, take off, and have your child tell you what he sees out the window as you travel. Be sure you have a specific destination in mind before you "buy" the ticket.

4. Make paper helicopters (page 158).

Books:

Airplanes, by David Peterson
Airports, by David Peterson

Poetry:

The First Book of Poetry, selected by Isabel J. Peterson
    "Aeroplane," by Mary McB. Green
For a Child, collected by Wilma McFarland
    "The Dirigible," by Ralph W. Bergengren
    "Airplanes," by Muriel Schulz

Zoo Animals

A zoo is a place where we can safely see wild animals. Large animals such as bears, lions, and elephants must be kept in cages because they are not safe to touch or to play with. The people at the zoo try to make the animals' cages much like their natural homes in the jungle or the forest.

Learning Activities:

1. Make a zoo (page 166).
2. Play animal charades (page 70).
3. Take a trip to the zoo. Point out the differences in the types of cages or confinements the different kinds of animals are in. Talk about how they are similar to the animals' natural homes. Also point out the different things the animals like to eat.

4. Learn the names of the baby animals. Tell your child that a baby elephant is a calf; a baby bear is a cub; a baby kangaroo is a joey; a baby lion is a cub; a baby deer is a fawn; and so on.

Books:

Wild Animals that Help People, by M. Walker
Noah's Ark, by Peter Spier
The Biggest Bear, by Lynd Ward
If I Ran the Zoo, by Dr. Seuss

Poetry:

The First Book of Poetry, selected by Isabel J. Peterson
    "Furry Bear," by A. A. Milne
    "Eletelephony," by Laura E. Richards
The Moon is Shining Bright as Day, edited by Ogden Nash
    "The Panther," by Ogden Nash
Toucans Two and Other Poems, by Jack Prelutsky
    "The Zebra"
    "The Hippopotamus"
    "The Polar Bear"

Dinosaurs

Dinosaurs hold a special fascination for children. They are somehow a link between reality and fantasy. Some concepts you'll want to review before teaching your child about dinosaurs are:

1. Dinosaurs are animals that lived millions of years ago on the earth.

2. There are no dinosaurs alive on the earth anymore.

3. We can learn about dinosaurs from their bones left in the ground.

4. We can learn the names of dinosaurs.

5. Some dinosaurs had pointed teeth. They ate meat. Other dinosaurs had flat teeth. They ate only plants.

6. Baby dinosaurs hatched from eggs.

Learning Activities:

1. You will be amazed at how quickly your child will pick up the names of dinosaurs. It is fun for them to be able to use such big words. Teach the names of the dinosaurs by giving clues like the following:

Tyrannosaurus   "The meanest . . ."
Diplodocus   "The longest . . ."
Brontosaurus   "The biggest . . ."
Brachiosaurus   "The fattest . . ."
Triceratops   "Three horns on his head . . ."
Pentaceratops   "Five horns on his head . . ."
Stegosaurus   "Plates on his back . . ."

2. Go to a museum to see dinosaur bones. Try to name the dinosaurs.

Most of your experience with dinosaurs will have to be through books. Four good ones are:

Dinosaur Time, by Peggy Parish
Dinosaurs, illustrated by Dot and Sy Barlowe
The Scholastic Fun Fact Book of Dinosaurs, published by Scholastic Book Services
Dinosaurs, by David Lambert

Farm Animals

There are many different kinds of animals on a farm. They supply us with much of our food and clothing. Farmers work hard to take good care of their animals.

Learning Activities:

1. See how many different farm animals your child can name.

2. When you use products that come from farm animals (eggs, milk, butter, wool, honey, etc.) ask your child where they come from. (Stress products that do not require loss of the animals' lives.)

3. Make arrangements to go to a farm when the chores are being done. Observe how the farmer cares for the animals and how the animals work for the farmer.

4. Observe cows being milked, sheep being sheared, honey being gathered, and so on.

5. If you and your child have a chance to see the birth of an animal, it would be a valuable experience.

6. Play "The Farmer in the Dell." (See the book list below.)

7. Learn the sounds the animals make by singing "Old MacDonald Had a Farm." (See the book list below.)

8. Learn the names of baby farm animals: a baby cow is a calf, a baby horse is a foal, a baby chicken is a chick, a baby goat is a kid, a baby pig is a piglet, a baby sheep is a lamb.

Books:

Charlie Needs a Cloak, by Tomie de Paola
A Calf Is Born, by Joanna Cole

Poetry:

The Moon Is Shining Bright as Day, edited by Ogden Nash
    "The Chicken"
    "The Duck," by Ogden Nash
A Child's Garden of Verses, by Robert Louis Stevenson
    "The Friendly Cow," by Robert Louis Stevenson

Songs:

Singing Bee! compiled by Jane Hart
"Old MacDonald Had a Farm"
"The Farmer in the Dell"
Eye Winker, Tom Tinker, Chin Chopper, by Tom Glazer
"The Barnyard Song"
"Five Little Ducks"
"The Little White Duck"
What Shall We Do and Allee Galloo! collected by Marie Winn
"When Ducks Get Up in the Morning"
"What Use Are You?"

Pets

Any tame animal that is kept just for fun as a special friend is called a pet. All pets need to be loved and cared for; they should be handled gently. Children should choose pets carefully because different pets have different needs, and some require more care than others.

Learning Activities:

1. If you are considering getting a pet for your child, be sure it is one that the child can care for so that you won't have to assume that responsibility.

2. Encourage your child to be loving and gentle in caring for and playing with his pet.

3. Explain carefully to your child how to care for his pet. Look in the library for a book on the care of the pet you have chosen.

4. Play "Who Am I?" (page 68). Describe a pet and have your child guess what it is (a cat, dog, goldfish, turtle, bird, gerbil). When he guesses correctly, ask, "If you had this pet, how would you take care of it?"

Books:

The Very Little Dog, by Grace Skaar
The Pet Show, by Ezra Jack Keats
Millions of Cats, by Wanda Gag
Pets, by Illa Podendorf

Poetry:

The Moon Is Shining Bright as Day, edited by Ogden Nash
    "Missing," by A. A. Milne
For a Child, collected by Wilma McFarland
    "Pet Show," by Arthur Guiterman
    "Chums," by Arthur Guiterman
    "To a Mischievous Kitten," by Frances Frost
    "My Dog," by Tom Robinson
Every Time I Climb a Tree, by David McCord
    "Scat! Scitten!"
    "Lost"

Fingerplays:

Let's Do Fingerplays, by Marion F. Grayson
    "Once I Saw a Bunny"

Songs:

Eye Winker, Tom Tinker, Chin Chopper, by Tom Glazer
    "There Was a Little Turtle"

Science

The following pages contain "mini-lessons" related to science. They can be used as a lesson in themselves or in connection with a related topic. For example, under the topic "Animals," activity number 6 (hatching eggs) could be used during your lessons on spring. Some useful equipment to have on hand for your science experiments includes a magnifying glass, magnets, a prism, a microscope, an egg incubator, a flashlight, a mirror, balloons, and a compass.

Encourage your child to be curious and to investigate things by letting him experiment with his environment. Curiosity is often mistaken for mischief. Ask your child questions about what he is doing and notice what kinds of questions your child asks most often. Are they permission questions: "Can I," or are they "how" and "why" questions? Remember, "Don't touch" often means "Don't learn."

In many cases firsthand experience is impossible. Vicarious experiences can be had through well-written books with large color photographs. Remember, however, that the best teacher is experience. The more senses a child can use, the more he will learn.

Air

These experiments teach that air is real and that air takes up space.

1. Place a paper towel inside a clear glass. Turn the glass upside down and lower it straight into a bowl of water. Why does the towel stay dry? Air takes up space in the glass and will not allow water to enter. Next, tilt the glass while it is underwater. Air bubbles will escape, and the glass will fill with water.

2. Blow up a balloon. Why does it get bigger? The air inside is stretching it. Air takes up space. Let the balloon go. The air inside will cause the balloon to fly. Air can move things.

What other things can air move? Observe clothes on a clothesline on a breezy day. Sit across the table from each other and blow a cottonball back and forth to each other.

3. Punch one hole in the top of a can. Try to pour out the liquid. It will come out very slowly if at all. Next, punch

another hole in the top of the can. The liquid will pour out quickly. The second hole lets air into the can. The air pushes the liquid out.

4. Tie a large handkerchief at four corners with string, forming a parachute. Tie a small toy man on the ends of the string. Throw the parachute up into the air. As it comes down, the parachute will fill with air and float down.

5. Air can make things float. Fill one balloon with water and another with air. Place both in a tub of water. Explain to your child that this is how boats float. Their shape allows them to hold a lot of air so that they can float.

6. Use a glass jar with a tight-fitting lid to show how a submarine works. Put the lid on the jar and float it in a tub of water. Then take the lid part-way off to allow water to enter and let the jar submerge.

7. Fire needs air to burn. Light a small candle and watch it burn for a few minutes. Then place a large jar over it. Time how long it takes for the fire to use up all the air and go out.

Light and Color

1. Place a mirror in a glass of water. Reflect sunlight off the mirror and onto a wall. You will get a rainbow on the wall. This shows that there is color in light. You may get the same effect from having sunlight shine through a prism onto a wall.

2. Make color jars. Take small glass jars (such as baby-food jars), fill them with water, and add a few drops of food coloring to each. Start with the primary colors. Line up the red jar and the yellow jar and look through them into the light. You will see orange. Repeat with the other jars.

3. Form the secondary colors by adding a drop of red to the yellow jar to form orange. Do this with the other primary colors. Always add a small amount of the darker color to a larger amount of the lighter color.

Water

Water can be liquid, but it can also be a solid or a gas.

1. Heat water to boiling. Observe the steam. Steam is water in the form of a gas.

2. Place a cup of water in the freezer and wait until it freezes. The water has become a solid.

3. Rub a wet sponge on each end of a blackboard. Shine a sun lamp on one side to speed up the evaporation. What happened to the water? Where did it go?

The sun shines on lakes, rivers, and oceans. The water evaporates into the air and forms clouds in the sky. When the clouds cool down, the steam turns back into water, and it rains.

4. Hold a glass filled with ice over a boiling pan of water. The steam will collect on the glass, form water droplets, and "rain" back into the pan.

Measurements

1. Size and weight are not necessarily related. Something big can be light. Something small can be heavy.

Have your child stand with his arms stretched out at shoulder level. Place a large plastic bag filled with styrofoam chips in one hand. Place a small desk paperweight in the other. (You may use any large light object and small heavy object to demonstrate this point.)

2. Fractions. Teach "whole," "half," and "quarter" by dividing an apple. Ask, "How many half apples are there in the whole apple? How many quarter apples are in the half? How many in the whole?" Next use measuring cups to show the same relationships. Ask, "How many of these half cups will it take to fill up this whole cup?" "How many quarter cups?"

Practice these concepts with water during bathtime, or with sand in the sandbox. Once these concepts are learned, let your child practice using them by helping with food preparation.

Animals

1. Watch a caterpillar spin a cocoon and develop into a butterfly.

2. Visit a farm and talk about the various products we get from the different animals.

3. Dig up some worms and put them into a jar. Watch them digging in the soil.

4. Collect and observe live insects.

5. Make an ant farm.

6. Get eggs from a poultry farm and watch them hatch.

7. Gather seashells on the beach and learn about the animals that once lived in them.

8. Observe the birth of an animal.

Plants

1. Plant a sponge garden. Place a clean (preferably new) sponge in a shallow pan with one inch of water. Sprinkle the top of the sponge with grass seed. Place the "garden" in

a warm, sunny spot. Continue to add enough water to keep the sponge wet. You will have sprouts in a couple of days.

2. Learn how plants drink. Fill a clear glass with water. Put enough red food coloring into the water to make the water quite red. Place a stick of celery into the water. After a day or two the red color will go up the stick of celery and into the leaves as the water is absorbed.

3. Learn how seeds grow. Plant a bean seed in a clear plastic cup. Place the cup in a warm, sunny place and water it frequently. As the seed begins to sprout, you will be able to see the roots through the cup.

4. Sprout wheat or beans. Cover the bottom of a canning jar with wheat or dried beans. Fill the jar half full with warm water. Let it stand overnight in a warm, dark place. In the morning, pour off the water and rinse the seeds well, pouring off all the excess water. Cover the jar with a loosely woven cloth (such as cheesecloth) secured with a rubber band, or punch holes in the flat lid of the canning jar. Rinse the seeds and drain off the excess water every morning and night until the sprouts are one or two inches long. Now they are ready to eat! Your sprouts can be stored in the refrigerator for three to four days.

5. Root an avocado or a sweet potato. Put three toothpicks into the sides of an avocado seed or a sweet potato, forming a ledge at the center of the seed. Rest these toothpicks on the rim of a glass filled with water. Allow the lower half of the seed to be immersed in water. As water is absorbed, continue adding water to cover the lower half of the seed. A beautiful plant will grow from the seed.

6. Learn the parts of a plant. Gather flowers and label their different parts: leaf, stamen, pistil, petal, and root.

7. Learn the edible parts of plants.
Leaves: lettuce, cabbage, spinach
Bud and flower: cauliflower, broccoli
Root: carrots, potato, radish, onion, beets

Seed: peas, corn, beans

Stalk: celery, asparagus, rhubarb

8. Discover the differences in the coverings of fruit.

Rough: pineapples, oranges, lemons

Hard: coconuts, nuts, melons

Smooth: apples, pears, watermelons, bananas

Soft: tomatoes, cherries, grapes, plums

9. Give your child a seed pod. Let him examine it and find the seeds.

10. Have a variety of seeds for your child to examine. Talk about the plants that will come from them. Match the seeds to pictures of the plant they will produce.

11. Transplant a plant. Look at the different parts of the plant and talk about the care they need.

12. Talk about the different products we get from trees.

13. Take the seeds out of a fruit (apple, pumpkin, orange or grapefruit), plant them, and watch them grow.

Weather

1. Make a large thermometer out of poster paper. Make the "mercury" movable so you can change it as the weather changes. Along the side of the thermometer, place pictures of the type of clothing that would be worn for that temperature. For example, near 85 degrees F., place a picture of a child in shorts or a sun dress; near 30 degrees F., have a picture of a child in a snowsuit. You may also wish to put seasonal symbols beside the temperature readings, such as a sun near 80 degrees and snowflakes near 25 degrees.

2. Listen to the weather forecast on television. Let your child move the "mercury" to the temperature that is forecast for the next day. Let him help decide what clothing would be appropriate to wear for the temperature forecasted.

3. Have a large thermometer outside of a window or door where your child can read it. Let him compare the temperature on the real thermometer with the forecast.

4. Provide a calendar for your child's room. Let him place a weather-symbol sticker (sun, cloud, rain, snow, wind) on each day according to the kind of weather you're having.

5. Make a weather chart. On a large piece of poster paper, make a circular chart of the seasons. A good symbol to use is a fruit tree. In the spring (at the top of your chart) the tree is in blossom. In the summer (on the right side of the chart) there is fruit on the tree. In the fall (at the bottom of the chart) the leaves on the tree are orange, gold, and red. In the winter (on the left side of the chart) the tree is bare. Your child can help make the chart by making the blossoms, fruit, and leaves for the trees. Print in large letters the name of the season next to the tree representing it.

Crystal Garden

Materials needed:
    Aluminum pie pans
    Porous materials: tanbark, driftwood, lava rock, cork, pieces of sponge, concrete chips, or charcoal briquets.
    Arrange the porous materials in the pie pans, piling them on each other to make a jumbled surface. Mix the following:

4 tablespoons iodized table salt
4 tablespoons liquid bluing
4 tablespoons water
1 tablespoon ammonia

Spoon the solution over the garden and then add one or two drops of food coloring. The garden will take several days to form.

Science Books

Moon, Sun and Stars, by John Lewellyn
Sea Monsters of Long Ago, by Millicent Selsam
Is This a Baby Dinosaur? by Millicent Selsam
Prove It, by Rose Wyler and Gerald Ames
Eat the Fruit, Plant the Seed, by Millicent Selsam
Seeds by Wind and Water, by J. Jordan
Follow the Wind, by Alvin Tresselt
　　Look for the series *A New True Book,* published by Children's Press. Some titles in that series are:
Plants We Know, by O. Irene Miner
Seeds and More Seeds, by Millicent Selsam
Egg to Chick, by Millicent Selsam
Baby Animals, by Illa Podendorf
Birds We Know, by Margaret Friskey
Air Around Us, by Margaret Friskey
　　The National Geographic Society publishes a wonderful series of books for children called *Books for Young Explorers.* They have beautiful large color photographs true to the *National Geographic* tradition and a simple text understandable even to the very young. Look for these in your library, or they can be purchased from the National Geographic Society.

Field Trips

　　Before going on a field trip, you will want to make arrangements with the management of the establishment. Most places are glad to show you and your child what they do. If there are specific things you want your child to learn (such as having a policeman talk about safety) be sure to specify this when you call and make arrangements for your visit. Some of our favorite places to visit on field trips are:

Fire station
Newspaper press
Building site
Daddy's work
Post office
Zoo
Pet shop
Police station
Library
Florist
Bakery
Dentist
Hospital
Farm
Hatchery (fish and chicken)
Museum (art and science)
Cannery
Airport
Cheese factory
Dairy
Aquarium

Look for the special attractions that your community has to offer, and take advantage of the educational opportunities in your area.

Learning Games

This chapter provides easy-to-follow instructions and patterns for making games, toys, and worksheets. These games can be used to reinforce the concepts described in chapter 1, or they can be used alone as separate activities. Included are individual activities for you and your child to do alone, as well as group games for those days when your home is the neighborhood gathering place. There are also five computer games written in BASIC, a language common to almost all home computers. These simple computer games are geared to preschoolers, teaching such concepts as up-down-right-left, telling time, spelling, adding, and developing memory skills. The section on toys gives instructions on how to make educational toys at very low cost.

The learning worksheets in this chapter were created on one of those boring days when my son Michael could find "nothing to do." He said, "Mommy, can you make me a game?" So I sat down with a pile of scratch paper and made worksheets like the ones you find here. Filling out these worksheets has become one of his favorite activities. These are only examples for you to use in making your own worksheets. They begin very simply.

There are workbooks available with activities similar to these worksheets, but making your own is more effective because you can make them to fit the level of learning of your own child.

Games

1. *What's Missing?* This is a memory game. It will help your child learn to be observant and to concentrate. Start with a few unlike objects, for example, a toy car, a small doll, and a block. Have your child look at the objects and then close his eyes while you take one away. Then he opens his eyes and guesses what's missing. The more alike the objects are and the more objects you have, the harder the game becomes. Remembering if the blue, yellow, or red block is missing is harder than remembering if the truck, pencil, or cup is missing. For the very young, start with three to five unlike objects and work up to several like objects as your child gets better at the game.

Objects to use: alphabet letters, numbers, colored blocks, animal cards, small toy animals, kitchen utensils, cars, trucks, dolls, a baby bottle, diaper pins, a rattle.

2. *Who (or What) Am I?* This is a riddle game. You say something like, "I'm red and round and juicy and sweet, and I grow on a tree. What am I?" Start with general clues and then go to more specific ones. Let your child guess as often as he wishes. Then let him have a turn asking the riddle, and you guess the answer from his clues.

3. *Follow Directions.* Give three simple commands, for example, pick up the book, hop to the table, put the book on the table. Give all of the commands before the child starts. This helps him learn how to listen and follow directions. Increase the difficulty of the directions as the child matures.

4. *Simon Says.* This game helps teach listening. If you say, "Simon says touch your nose," your child should follow the instruction and touch his nose. If you just say "touch your nose," he shouldn't do it. Tell your child he should do only what Simon says. Let him take a turn being Simon.

5. *Mother, May I?* This game is similar to Simon Says except that the child is trying to reach a goal by moving a certain distance, such as crossing the room. When you give the child a command such as "Take three giant steps forward," he must reply "Mother, may I?" before he takes the steps. If he fails to say it, he has to return to the starting position. Other possible steps are baby steps, kangaroo hops, somersaults, twirling, and skipping.

6. *I Spy with My Little Eye.* Choose an object you both can see, for example, a red stocking. Say, "I spy with my little eye something that is red." Your child guesses all of the red things he can find until he guesses the stocking. Then it's his turn to "spy" something while you guess. This is a good game to play while traveling in the car. You can also use letters, numbers, or shapes as well as colors. This game can be played by a group of children with each one taking a turn to guess.

7. *Story Problems.* Make up your own simple mathematical story problems for your child to solve. For example (using pictures to illustrate), you may say, "A farmer had three lambs. His neighbor gave him one more lamb. How many lambs does he have now?"

8. *Will It Float or Sink?* In the summer, play this game outside in a wading pool; in the winter you can play it in the bathtub. Obtain many different objects, such as a spoon, a plastic toy, a nail, and a large block of wood. Ask your child if each object will float or sink. Then let him try it.

9. *Water Play.* Let your child play in his bath or in a wading pool with many different kinds of objects. There are many valuable experiences a child can gain through water play. Try some of these objects in his bath: sponges, small pitchers, a medicine dropper, a handturned egg beater (not electric!) and liquid soap, straws to blow through, a funnel, plastic squeeze bottles, rubber balls.

Group Games

1. *Color Relays.* Divide the children into three or more even groups. Give each child a color badge, each group having the same color. Outline a starting line and a finishing line. Then give each group different instructions for finishing. Say, for example, "All the children with a yellow badge, hop on one foot." When the yellow group is finished, you may say, "All the children with blue badges, gallop like a horse." Continue in that manner. Be sure to emphasize that being first to finish is not important; all children who finish are winners.

2. *Animal Charades.* Have the children sit in a large circle. The first child will come to you and look at a picture of an animal he will imitate. He can make the sound of the animal or use any movement he thinks will help the other children guess. (There are no teams in this game; the children are not competing.) My neighbors' daughter Marilee was shown a picture of a kangaroo, so she ran over to the dolls, held one on her tummy, and started to hop! The other children loved it!

3. *Red Light, Green Light.* Make two four-inch circles cut from red and green construction paper. These will be your traffic lights. Have all the children line up at the starting line. Let one child be "it" and operate the lights. When he holds up the green circle, he calls out "green light," and all of the children can run until he holds up the red circle and says "red light"; then all of the children must freeze. Anyone who keeps going on a red light must go back to the starting position. Let each child have a turn being "it."

4. *Bounce the Bear.* Spread a double-bed–sized flat sheet out on the floor. Have the children stand around the outside of the sheet, holding onto the edge of the sheet with both hands and lifting it off the floor. Practice lifting the sheet up and pulling it down together. Once the children have the rhythm of the up-and-down motion, place a large

teddy bear in the middle and have the children try to bounce him off the sheet. Next, use a small teddy bear and see how much higher he will bounce! This game is guaranteed to be a favorite!

5. *Jack-Be-Nimble.* Build a candlestick out of building blocks, placing a thick dowel on the top for the candle. Have the children stand in a circle around the candle. Using each child's own name in the place of "Jack," sing, for example, "Greg be nimble, Greg be quick, Greg jump over the candlestick." Then the child tries to jump over the blocks without knocking them over. Have all of the children sing and clap as they await their own turn to jump.

6. *I Have a Little Doggie.* Have the children sit in a circle on the floor. The child who is "it" walks around the outside of the circle holding a small stuffed dog (or a beanbag). He touches each child softly on the head as he says, "I have a little doggie, and he won't bite you, and he won't bite you . . . but he will bite *you!*" He drops the doggie behind that child and runs around the circle while the other child chases him. If he can reach the vacant spot before the child he touched, he sits down in the circle in that spot. Then the new child becomes "it."

7. *Duck, Duck, Goose.* This game is similar to "I Have a Little Doggie," except that the child who is "it" says "duck, duck, duck" until he reaches the child he wants; then he says "goose" as he drops the bean bag and runs.

8. *Red Rover.* Divide the children into two groups. Have each group form a single line, holding hands and facing the other team. The first team calls out, "Red rover, red rover, send Nickie right over." Nickie runs and tries to break through the line of the team that called her. If she does break through, she gets to choose someone from that team to go back to her team with her. If she does not break through, she has to stay on the team that called her over.

9. *Popcorn.* Have the children curl up into a ball on the floor, pretending to be kernels of popcorn. You say, "I'm turning on the stove. The pan is getting warm. Now it's getting hot; very hot! Those little kernels are starting to move. Pretty soon they're going to pop!" The children will be anxious to "pop" and so will probably start jumping up as soon as you turn on the stove! Encourage them to be patient, remembering how real popcorn has to sizzle for a while before it's ready to pop.

10. *Seeds.* A variation to "Popcorn" is to have the children pretend to be seeds. You go around and "water" the seeds and be the sun shining on the seeds. Pretty soon the seeds start to sprout. They grow so slowly, bigger and bigger. Be sure to ask each child what kind of plant he is.

11. *Hot Potato.* Have the children sit in a circle on the floor. Pass the "potato"—a small ball or a beanbag—around the circle while music is playing. The object is to not have the beanbag when the music stops. (For older children, the game is played by eliminating the child from the circle if he is caught with the potato when the music stops. I would not recommend this for preschoolers, as a young child may interpret his being "out" as a punishment for doing something wrong.)

12. *Wiggles.* Have the children stand in a large circle with you in the middle. Chant the following verse while everyone does what it says:

> Touch your head, head, head
> Shoulders, shoulders, shoulders
> Knees, knees, knees
> Toes, toes, toes
> Touch your nose!

(Repeat this two or three times until the children have the sequence well established, then continue.)

> Now turn around
> And touch the ground.
> Stand up!

And wiggle, and jiggle, and
wiggle, and jiggle . . .
And *freeze!*
March in place. (March, lifting
knees and elbows high.)
Now lean right, and left, and
right, and left. (Do this slowly.
Then start over.)

13. *Color Rounds.* Make large colored circles out of construction paper, at least two circles of each color you are using. Tape these in a large circle on the floor. The person who is "it" calls out a color, and the children sitting on that color jump up and change places with someone else who has his color. The person who is "it" can call out more than one color at a time. Then the children can choose any circle that is not occupied.

14. *What Time Is It, Mr. Fox?* The child who is "it" is Mr. Fox. The other children ask, "What time is it, Mr. Fox?" Mr. Fox answers "jumping time" or "hopping time" or "skipping time," and so on. The children do what Mr. Fox says and continue to ask, "What time is it Mr. Fox?" When Mr. Fox says, "It's dinner time!" all of the children run to a predetermined "home." Anyone Mr. Fox tags before the child reaches home helps him tag other children. The last one tagged is the new Mr. Fox.

15. *Back to Back.* The child who is "it" calls out, "Back to back." All of the children find a partner and back up to him. "It" calls out, "Face to face" or "shake hands" or "toe to toe" or "touch elbows," and so on. Each time the children find a new partner. Use an odd number of children, and each time a new call is made, the child without the partner calls the next command.

Musical Group Games

In the following books, you will find music and instructions for musical group games listed:

Singing Bee! compiled by Jane Hart
   "The Farmer in the Dell"
   "The Mulberry Bush"
   "Bluebird"
   "Go Round and Round the Village"
   "London Bridge"
   "Looby Loo"

Do Your Ears Hang Low? by Tom Glazer
   "The Hoky Poky"

Look for more group games in chapter 5, "Physical Activities."

Toys

1. Glue a circle of colored felt in the bottom of each cup of a muffin tin. Collect different sizes of colored craft pom-poms (available at craft stores). Using a pair of tongs, have your child place the red pom-poms in the red cup, the blue pom-poms in the blue cup, and so on. The tongs are important for developing coordination and concentration skills.

This toy can also be made with numbers by gluing a number in the bottom of the cup and having your child put three buttons (or beans) in the "3" cup, and so on.

2. Use empty pop bottles and the rubber sealers from wide-mouth jars for a ring toss.

3. Plastic two-liter pop bottles make good bowling pins. Use any large rubber ball to knock them down.

4. Make sewing cards from the covers of old coloring books or picture books, or laminate a picture to poster board. Punch holes outlining the picture. Use yarn to sew

around the holes. (Put a piece of masking tape around the end of the yarn to facilitate sewing.)

5. Using a large sheet of canvas, plastic, or poster board, make a map of your neighborhood for playing cars. On your map include your house, your child's best friend's house, your child's favorite eating place, your church, big sister's school, the grocery store, daddy's work place—all the important places for your child.

6. Make an alphabet mat from a large piece of canvas or heavy plastic (six feet by five feet) divided into one-foot squares. (Black electrical tape makes good dividing lines.) Inside each square place (in random order) a nine-inch capital letter. These can be made from felt and sewn on, or you can purchase large stick-on letters from educational supply stores. (You will have thirty squares, so four letters will be repeated).

To play on the mat, hold up a letter flash card, have your child tell you the name of the letter, make the letter's sound, find the letter on the mat, and stand on it. Use both uppercase and lowercase-letter flash cards.

You can also play a sound-guessing game with the mat. Say, "I'm thinking of a letter that says 'kuh'." Your child finds the K and stands on it.

7. Play alphabet twister. Using either of the above two methods for finding letters, have your child place his right foot on one letter, left foot on another, right hand on another, and so on.

8. Play Color Bingo. Using poster board, make lap boards one foot square. With permanent marking pens, divide the board into nine equal squares (four inches each). In each square, make a circle that is about one and a half inches in diameter. Color each circle with a permanent marking pen. I use the primary colors (red, yellow, and blue), the secondary colors (orange, green, and purple), and white, black, and brown.

To play Color Bingo, say, "I'm thinking of a color that is warm. I've seen birds and flowers this color." If your child guesses something like "blue" at this point, remind him you are thinking of a warm color and that blue is a cool color (see lesson on colors, page 8). If he guesses red, say, "Red is a warm color, but it's not the one I'm thinking of." Then go on to more specific clues, such as, "It's the color of lemons, butter, and the sun." When he guesses yellow, he gets to put a marker on his yellow circle. Continue until the whole board is covered.

Using the same pattern as described above, you may also make number and letter bingo cards.

9. On 4-by-6-inch recipe cards, stencil the numbers one through ten, each number on a single card. Make a matching dot card for each number card by putting colored three-quarter-inch stick-on dots on cards. (These dot stickers are available where office and school supplies are sold.)

Have your child place the dot cards out of sequence on a floor or table. Then have him place the corresponding number card on top of each dot card.

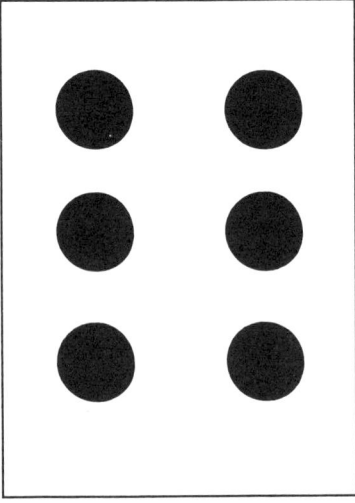

Learning Worksheets

1. Draw a line connecting the capital letters that are the same.

A	**C**
D	**B**
B	**E**
E	**A**
C	**D**

2. Draw a line matching the uppercase letter to its corresponding lowercase letter.

B	**c**
D	**a**
A	**e**
C	**b**
E	**d**

3. Circle the capital letter on the line that matches the capital letter in the box.

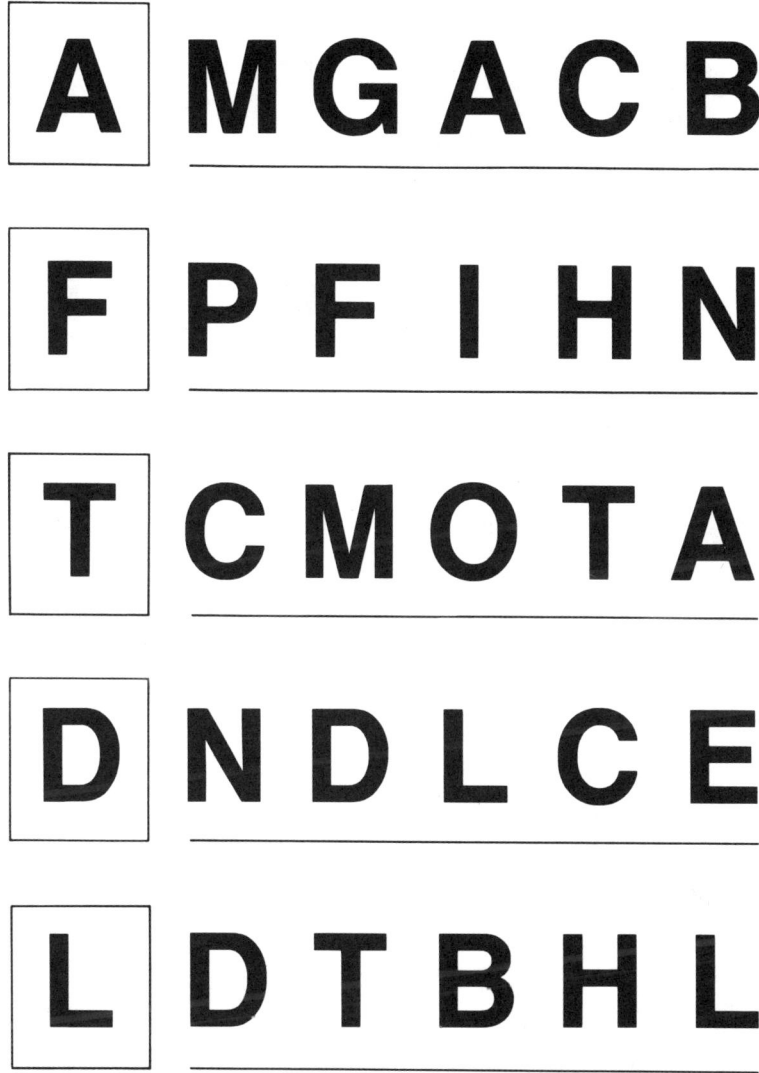

4. Circle the lowercase letter on the line that matches the letter in the box.

| o | b p e o c |

| f | t k f r h |

| u | m n w y u |

| s | c z s o a |

| m | n u j m r |

5. Draw a line from the objects to the corresponding numerals.

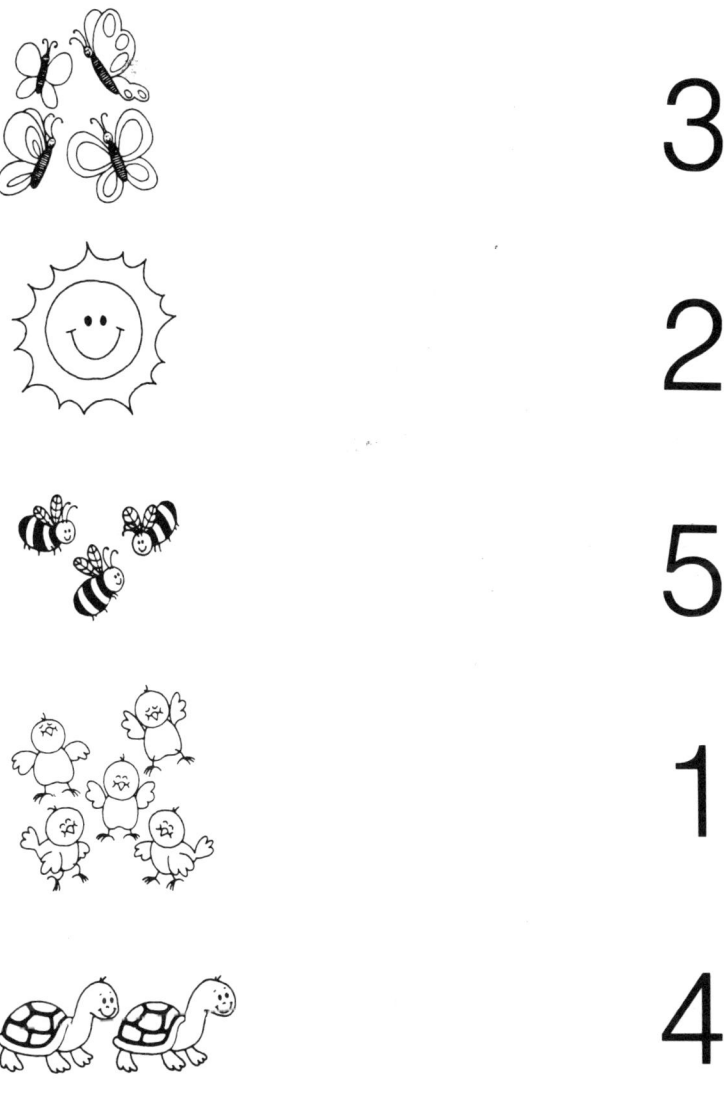

6. Draw a line between the two colors that are the same.

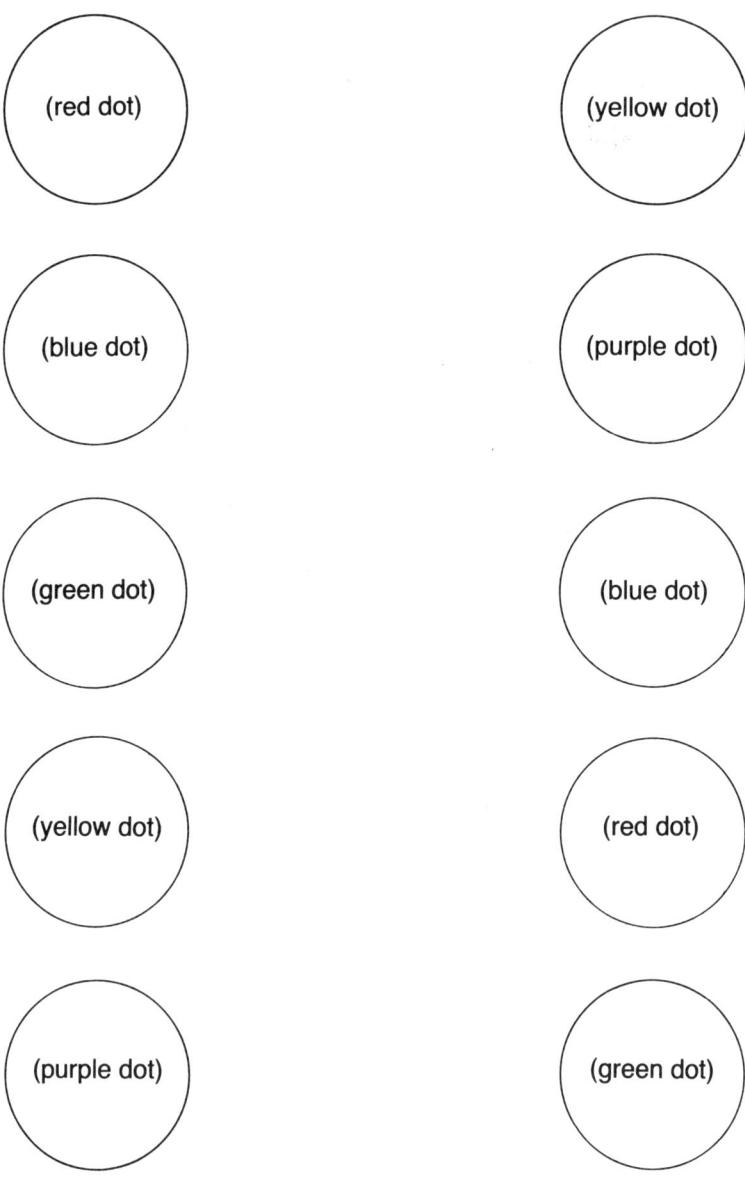

7. Read the word and color the circle.

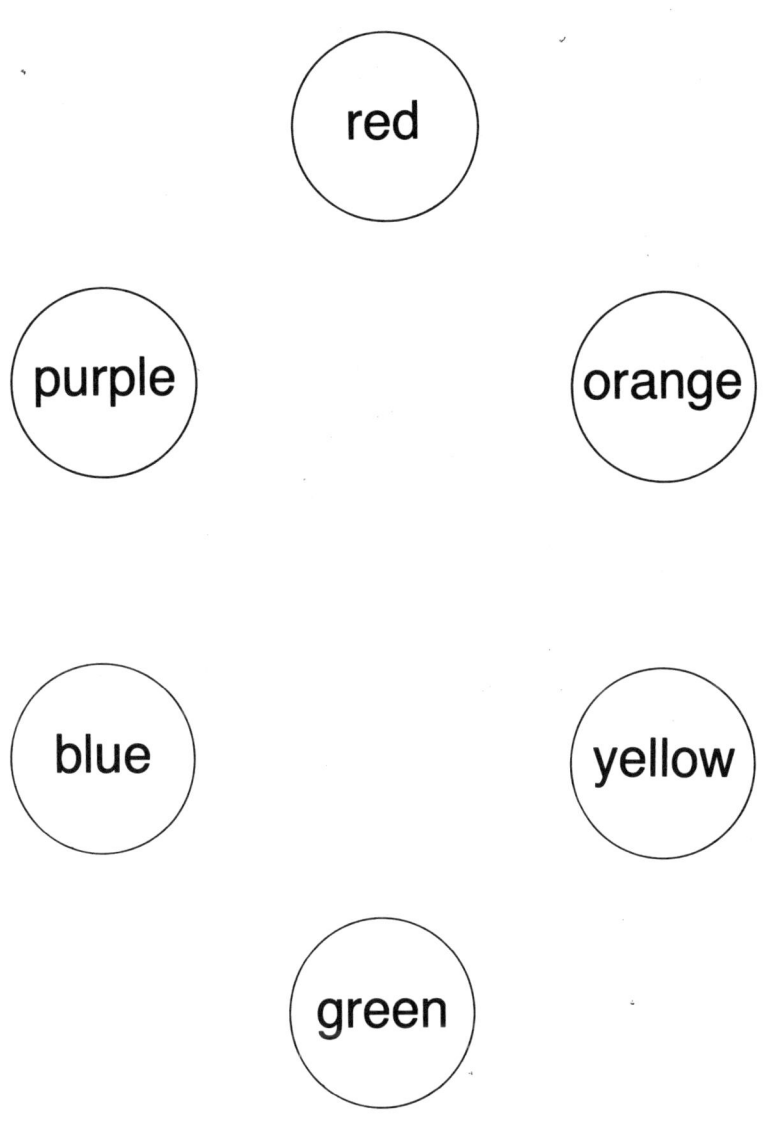

8. Follow the dots to form each capital letter. Practice making more letters on the lines provided.

A   _____   _____   _____

B   _____   _____   _____

C   _____   _____   _____

D   _____   _____   _____

E   _____   _____   _____

9. Follow the dots to form each lowercase letter. Practice making more letters on the lines provided.

m   ____   ____   ____

n   ____   ____   ____

o   ____   ____   ____

p   ____   ____   ____

q   ____   ____   ____

r   ____   ____   ____

10. Follow the dots to form each number. Practice making more numbers on the lines provided.

1   _____   _____   _____

2   _____   _____   _____

3   _____   _____   _____

4   _____   _____   _____

5   _____   _____   _____

11. Read the word. Draw a line from the word to the arrow that is doing what the word says.

over

through

up

right

down

left

12. Look at the picture. Write the word. (In the beginning, fill in the last two letters, for example, "—AT," and have your child fill in only the "B." Use as many rhyming pictures as you can think of so all your child has to do is change the first letter. Soon he will be able to fill in all of the letters by himself.)

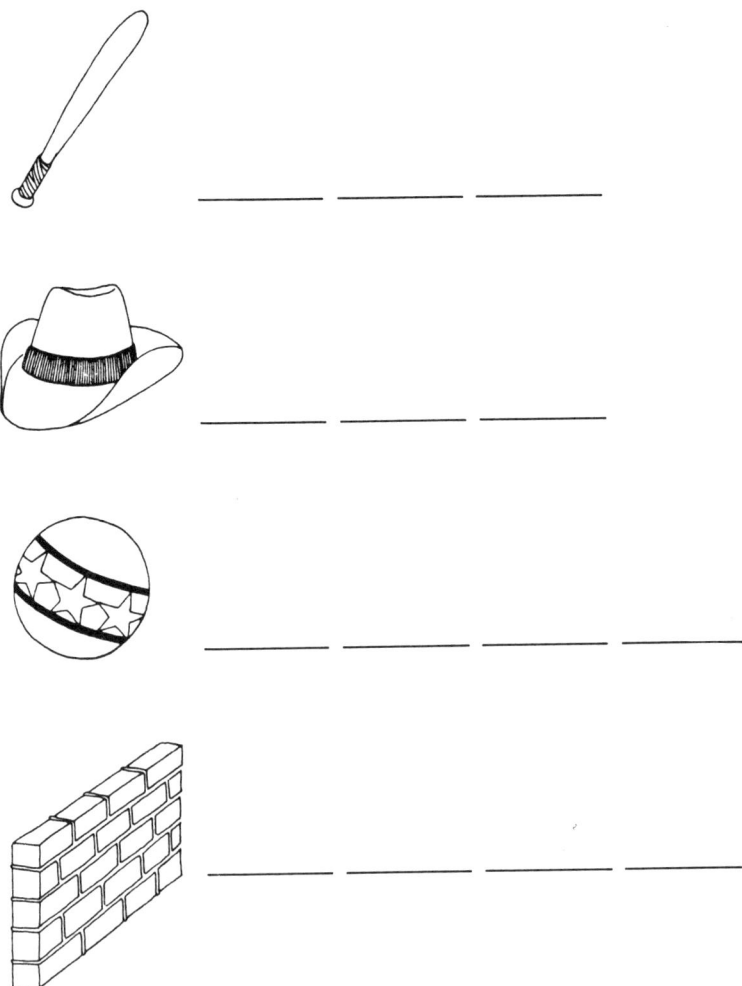

13. Write the lowercase letter on the line next to its uppercase letter.

A ____ G ____

B ____ H ____

C ____ I ____

D ____ J ____

E ____ K ____

F ____ L ____

14. Write the uppercase letter on the line next to its lowercase letter.

a ___   g ___

b ___   h ___

c ___   i ___

d ___   j ___

e ___   k ___

f ___   l ___

15. Draw a line from the number word to the numeral.

six	**1**
four	**7**
one	**4**
ten	**6**
eight	**10**
seven	**8**

16. Read the number word. Practice drawing the numeral on the lines.

three _____ _____ _____

six _____ _____ _____

two _____ _____ _____

five _____ _____ _____

seven _____ _____ _____

four _____ _____ _____

one _____ _____ _____

eight _____ _____ _____

ten _____ _____ _____

nine _____ _____ _____

17. Circle the two words on the line that are the same.

man   hit   man

hall   fan   fan

sit   sit   fan

call   fat   call

cat   cat   mall

fat   mall   mall

18. Circle the two words on the line that rhyme.

sit	fan	hit
hall	mall	far
sit	car	far
tall	cat	hall
cat	sat	hill
cat	fan	man

19. Read the word. Draw a line to the color.

red

(purple dot)

orange

(yellow dot)

yellow

(blue dot)

green

(red dot)

blue

(green dot)

purple

(orange dot)

20. Draw a line matching the mother animal to her baby.

21. Draw a line from the shape to the first sound in its name.

S

R

T

O

22. Draw a circle *on* the house.
    Make an X *in* the circle.
    Draw a box *beside* the house.
    Write your name *under* the box.
    Draw a picture of yourself *between* the trees.

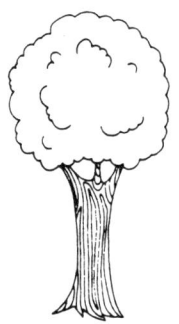

23. Match the animal to what it gives us.

24. Match the animal with its home.

Computer Games

If you are the owner of a computer, chances are you'd like to use it to help teach your preschooler. Some computers are built mainly for playing games; others are designed more for business applications. However, either type of computer can be used to develop and play simple games in the BASIC language, which is common to almost all computers. And while there are many educational computer games on the market, it is often more fun and certainly less expensive to develop your own simple games for your child. If you're not that ambitious but would still like to save money, there are many books available that contain games written in BASIC that you can key into your computer. A visit to your local bookstore will reveal the large number of books available. Some simple games are presented below to illustrate the kinds of games that can be written and played even on business computers with very little effort.

Before presenting the computer codes for the games, some general words of advice and explanation are in order. The programs presented here were written on an Osborne Computer in MBASIC (© Microsoft Computer Corporation), which is commonly used with the CP/M operating system. As you are probably aware, different computers use different versions of BASIC. The BASIC language on your computer may differ in some commands from those presented here, so if you don't have MBASIC, you may need to adapt some of the command lines to your BASIC syntax. An attempt has been made to minimize this problem by using only the simplest programming commands common to most versions of BASIC. The logic of the programs should be valid under any circumstance. If problems arise, consult your user's manual or your local computer users' group.

Part of the fun of the learning programs presented in this chapter involves making use of any screen graphics capabilities your computer may have. Having the computer make a noise and some interesting patterns on the screen when the child gets a right answer can help hold his attention longer and make learning more fun. There is a price to be paid for these features, however, in the amount of programming involved. Usually the logic required to make the game work is a small effort compared to designing and executing enjoyable graphics designs. In the programs presented here, some relatively simple graphics routines are offered using normal characters, not specialized graphics characters. You have the option of including these routines, leaving them out if you don't want to do all that typing, or substituting your own clever routines if you get bitten by the computer bug. Beware of the last option, however—programming graphics for your child can be addicting!

Note that the documentation to help you follow the program logic is presented at the right side of the page. *You should not key this material into the computer.* Within the program are a few remarks (statements that begin with ') to assist those who wish to modify the program. You need not key these in if you do not wish to.

Here are some notes about particular programming features of the games that may be useful to you:

1. Some of the game programs require the generation of random numbers. The method used here is the command RANDOMIZE to request from the user a seed number to initialize the generator, followed by use of RND to represent the random number. Your BASIC language may have a different or more sophisticated method for generating random numbers. If you use the method suggested here, be sure to enter a different random number seed each time you play. Otherwise, you'll get the same sequence every time.

2. Some game programs use the INPUT$( ) function. An example is X$=INPUT$(1), which would set X$ equal to the next character entered (no carriage return required). If your BASIC doesn't permit the INPUT function, use an INPUT command, or consult your manual for an appropriate substitute.

3. All the programs use the following command to clear the screen: PRINT CHR$(26). The ASCII character to clear the screen on our computer is number 26. Use the appropriate number for your computer. Alternatively, your BASIC may have a different clear screen command.

4. All the programs use the following command to position the cursor on the screen:

PRINT CHR$(27); " = ";CHR$(32 +X);CHR$(32 +Y);

The ASCII character for ESCAPE on our computer is number 27. The form of this command may vary from one computer to another. Or, your BASIC may have a different command for positioning the cursor. Consult your manual.

The Remember Game

In the Remember Game, the computer presents the player with a sequence of numbers of ever-increasing length, and the player must repeat back the sequence. The sequence is longer by one number with each turn, and play stops when the player makes his first mistake. For example, the computer may begin with "8," then blank the screen and say "Your turn." The player then enters "8." The computer then displays "8," blanks the screen, displays "2," blanks the screen, and says "Your turn." The player must enter "8," then "2," and so on. Eventually the sequence becomes so long that the player makes a mistake; the computer then displays "You blew it!" along with the correct sequence and the player's score, which is the length of the sequence correctly entered. This game is designed to help increase memory skills, number recognition skills, and concentration skills.

Source Code to be Keyed into the computer: ¦ Documentation:

```
1 ' The Remember Game              ¦
2 ' !!!!!!!!!!!!!!!!!!!!            ¦
20 GOSUB 500                       ¦ Clear screen
30 X=5 : Y=30 : GOSUB 600          ¦ Position cursor
40 PRINT "THE REMEMBER GAME"       ¦
50 X=10 : Y=12 : GOSUB 600         ¦
60 RANDOMIZE                       ¦ Request random number seed
70 DIM NUM(50)                     ¦ NUM contains the number sequence
                                   ¦   (up to 50)
100 FOR NGAME=1 TO 1000            ¦ Play up to 1000 times
110   FOR N=1 TO 50                ¦ Loop to generate number sequence
120     NUM(N) = INT(RND!10)       ¦
130     FOR M=1 TO N               ¦ Loop to display sequence
140       GOSUB 500                ¦
150       X=11 : Y=40 : PRINT NUM(M)  ¦
160       FOR AA=1 TO 500 : NEXT AA   ¦ Wait between numbers
170     NEXT M                     ¦
180     GOSUB 500                  ¦
190     X=10 : Y=36 : GOSUB 600    ¦
200     PRINT "YOUR TURN"          ¦
210     FOR GM=1 TO N              ¦ Loop to input player's sequence
220       GUESS$ = INPUT$(1)       ¦ Input each number to GUESS
```

```
230        IF INT(VAL(GUESS$)) <> NUM(GM)  ! Test each GUESS; if wrong, go to
_          THEN GOSUB 700 : GOTO 280       !    You-Blew-It subroutine and
                                           !    start again

240     NEXT GM                            !

250     FOR AA=1 TO 400 : NEXT AA          ! Wait to begin sequence display

260     NEXT N                             !

270     FOR AA=1 TO 400 : NEXT AA          ! Wait to start next game

280 NEXT NGAME                             !

499 ' ==================================   !

500 ' Subroutine to clear the screen       !

501 ' ==================================   !

510 PRINT CHR$(26)                         ! Clear screen

520 RETURN                                 !

599 ' ==================================   !

600 ' Subroutine to position the cursor    !

601 ' ==================================   !

610 PRINT CHR$(27) ; "=" ; CHR$(32+X)      ! Position cursor at line X,
    CHR$(32+Y);                            !    column Y

620 RETURN                                 !

699 ' ==================================   !

700 ' Subroutine "You-Blew-It"             !

701 ' ==================================   !

710 GOSUB 500                              !

720 PRINT CHR$(7)                          ! Ring bell

730 X=8 : Y=35 : GOSUB 600                 !
```

```
740 PRINT "YOU BLEW IT!"                 !

750 X=10 : Y=36 : GOSUB 600              !

760 PRINT "SCORE = " ; N-1               ! Score is the number of numbers

                                         !    successfully repeated

770 X=15 : Y=20 : GOSUB 600              !

780 PRINT "CORRECT SEQUENCE: ";          !

790 FOR AA=1 TO N-1                      ! Loop to print correct sequence

800    PRINT NUM(AA);                    !

810 NEXT AA                              !

820 X=20 : Y=30 : GOSUB 600              !

830 INPUT "HIT RETURN TO PLAY AGAIN", AA ! AA is a dummy variable

840 RETURN                               !
```

Note: The program will run if only the above part is keyed in. The following optional segment draws the numerals 1-9 in large size on the screen as the computer displays the sequence.

```
10 GOSUB 2000                            !

150        GOSUB 1000                    ! This statement replaces

                                         !    statement 150 above

899 ' ==================================  !

900 ' Subroutine to print Z at X+6,Y+34  ! To help center the numerals

901 ' ==================================  !

910 PRINT CHR$(27) ; "=" ; CHR$(38+X) ;  ! Position cursor and print Z$

    CHR$(66+Y);Z$                        !

920 RETURN                               !
```

```
999 ' ================================== ¦

1000 ' Subroutine to draw the numerals    ¦

1001 ' ================================== ¦

1010 Z$ = RIGHT$(STR$(NUM(M)*11),2)       ¦ Z$ is 22 for 2, 33 for 3, etc

1020 IF NUM(M)=0 THEN Z$="00"             ¦

1030 CC = NUM(M)                          ¦

1040 IF NUM(M)=0 THEN CC=10               ¦ For addressing the appropriate
                                          ¦    elements in the data arrays
                                          ¦    to draw the numerals

1050 FOR AA=1 TO NT(CC)                   ¦ Loop to call up the X and Y

1060    X = XP(CC,AA)                     ¦    coordinates from the data

1070    Y = YP(CC,AA)                     ¦    arrays and print each picture

1080    GOSUB 900                         ¦    element

1090 NEXT AA                              ¦

1100 RETURN                               ¦

1999 ' ================================== ¦

2000 ' Subroutine to read numeral patterns ¦

2001 ' ================================== ¦

2010 DIM NT(10) , XP(10,24) , YP(10,24)   ¦

2020 FOR AA=1 TO 10                       ¦ Loop to read values of NT, the

2030    READ NT(AA)                       ¦    number of picture elements in

2040 NEXT AA                              ¦    each numeral drawing

2050 DATA 12,19,19,19,21,23,15,24,22,24   ¦ Values of NT for 1234567890

2060 FOR AA=1 TO 10                       ¦ Loop to read data for X and Y

2080    FOR BB=1 TO NT(AA)                ¦    coordinates for each element
```

```
2090      READ XP(AA,BB),YP(AA,BB)        :  X(1,BB) contains the X (line

                                          :    number) coordinates for the

                                          :    picture elements for numeral

                                          :    "1"; X(2,BB) for numeral "2",

                                          :    etc. Y(1,BB) contains the

2100     NEXT BB                          :    Y (column) coordinates

2110 NEXT AA                              :

2120 DATA 2,4,1,5,2,5,3,5,4,5,5,5,6,5,7,5 :  X and Y values for "1"

2122 DATA 8,5,9,5,10,4,10,6               :

2130 DATA 3,1,2,1,1,2,1,4,1,6,1,8,2,9,3,9 :  ... for "2"

2135 DATA 4,9,5,7,6,5,7,3,8,1,9,1,10,1,10,3 :

2140 DATA 10,5,10,7,10,9                  :

2150 DATA 2,1,1,2,1,4,1,6,1,8,2,9,3,9,4,8 :  ... for "3"

2155 DATA 5,6,5,4,6,8,7,9,8,9,9,9,10,8,10,6 :

2160 DATA 10,4,10,2,9,1                   :

2170 DATA 2,1,3,1,4,1,5,1,6,1,6,3,6,5,6,7 :  ... for "4"

2175 DATA 6,9,1,5,2,5,3,5,4,5,5,5,6,5,7,5 :

2180 DATA 8,5,9,5,10,5                    :

2190 DATA 1,9,1,7,1,5,1,3,1,1,2,1,3,1,4,1 :  ... for "5"

2195 DATA 5,1,5,3,5,5,5,7,6,8,7,9,8,9,9,8 :

2200 DATA 10,7,10,5,10,3,10,2,9,1         :

2210 DATA 1,9,1,7,1,5,1,3,2,2,3,1,4,1,5,1 :  ... for "6"

2215 DATA 6,1,7,1,8,1,9,1,10,2,10,4,10,6  :

2220 DATA 10,8,9,9,8,9,7,9,6,8,5,7,5,5,5,3 :

2230 DATA 2,1,1,1,1,3,1,5,1,7,1,9,2,9,3,9 :  ... for "7"
```

```
2240 DATA 4,8,5,7,6,6,7,5,8,4,9,3,10,2      :

2250 DATA 1,2,1,4,1,6,1,8,2,9,3,9,4,8,5,7   : ... for "8"

2260 DATA 5,5,5,3,6,2,7,1,8,1,9,2,10,3,10,5 :

2270 DATA 10,7,9,8,8,9,7,9,6,8,4,2,3,1,2,1  :

2280 DATA 5,9,5,7,5,5,5,3,4,2,3,1,2,1,1,2   : ... for "9"

2285 DATA 1,4,1,6,1,8,2,9,3,9,4,9,5,9,6,9   :

2290 DATA 7,9,8,9,9,8,10,7,10,5,10,3        :

2300 DATA 1,2,1,4,1,6,1,8,2,9,3,9,4,9,5,9   : ... for "0"

2305 DATA 6,9,7,9,8,9,9,9,10,8,10,6,10,4,10 :

2310 DATA 2,9,1,8,1,7,1,6,1,5,1,4,1,3,1,2,1 :

2320 RETURN                                 :

3000 END                                    :
```

The Clock Game

The Clock Game is designed to help a child learn to tell time. A clock face is drawn on the screen displaying random times, and the child must enter the correct time. The game may be played on four levels of skill: whole hours only; whole hours and half hours; whole, half, and quarter hours; or every five minutes. It is recommended that one skill level be mastered before the next is attempted.

```
1   'The Clock Game                  :

2   '!!!!!!!!!!!!!!!                  :

9   'Read the clock face coordinates :

10 DIM XFACE(12),YFACE(12)           : Arrays for clock number

20 FOR AA=1 TO 12                    :     coordinates: XFACE for line,

30    READ XFACE(AA),YFACE(AA)       :     YFACE for column
```

```
40 NEXT AA                              :

50 DATA 4,47,7,53,11,57,15,53,18,47,19,39  : X, Y coordinates for "1",

60 DATA 18,31,15,25,11,21,7,24,4,31,3,39   :    "2", etc

99 'Read the big hand coordinates       :

100 DIM NPBIG(12),XBIG(12,7),YBIG(12,7) : NPBIG holds number of points for

110 FOR AA=1 TO 12                      :    each big hand; XBIG and YBIG

120    READ NPBIG(AA)                   :    hold coordinates for each

130 NEXT AA                             :    point

140 FOR AA=1 TO 12                      :

150    FOR BB=1 TO NPBIG(AA)            :

160       READ XBIG(AA,BB) , YBIG(AA,BB)  : Read coordinates

170    NEXT BB                          :

180 NEXT AA                             :

190 DATA 7,5,7,5,7,7,7,5,7,5,7,7        : NPBIG values for big hand to 1,

191 '                                   :    2, etc

200 DATA 11,40,10,41,9,42,8,43,7,44,6,45  : X, Y coordinates for big hand

205 DATA 5,46                           :    to 1

210 DATA 11,40,10,43,9,46,8,49,7,52     : ... to 2

230 DATA 11,42,11,44,11,46,11,48,11,50  : ... to 3

240 DATA 11,52,11,54                    :

250 DATA 11,40,12,43,13,46,14,48,15,52  : ... to 4

270 DATA 12,40,13,41,14,42,15,43,16,44  : ... to 5

280 DATA 17,45,18,46                    :

290 DATA 12,39,13,39,14,39,15,39,16,39  : ... to 6

300 DATA 17,39,18,39                    :
```

```
310 DATA 12,38,13,37,14,36,15,35,16,34    !  ... to 7

320 DATA 17,33,18,32                      !

330 DATA 11,38,12,35,13,32,14,29,15,26    !  ... to 8

350 DATA 11,36,11,34,11,32,11,30,11,28    !  ... to 9

360 DATA 11,26,11,24                      !

370 DATA 11,38,10,35,9,32,8,29,7,26       !  ... to 10

390 DATA 11,38,10,37,9,36,8,35,7,34,6,33  !  ... to 11

395 DATA 5,32                             !

400 DATA 10,39,9,39,8,39,7,39,6,39,5,39,4,39! ... to 12

401 '                                     !

500 'Determine the little hand coordinates !  Different from big hand

                                          !    coordinates only when

                                          !    past the half hour

580 DIM XLITOF(12,3),YLITOF(12,3)         !  X, Y coordinates for little hand

590 FOR AA=1 TO 12                        !    pointing between numbers

600    FOR BB=1 TO 3                      !

610       READ XLITOF(AA,BB),YLITOF(AA,BB) !

620    NEXT BB                            !

630 NEXT AA                               !

640 DATA 10,40,9,42,8,44                  !  Coordinates for little hand to

                                          !    after 1

650 DATA 11,40,10,45,9,50                 !  ... to after 2

660 DATA 11,40,12,45,13,50                !  ... to after 3

670 DATA 12,40,13,43,14,45                !  ... to after 4

680 DATA 12,39,14,40,16,41                !  ... to after 5
```

```
690 DATA 12,39,14,38,16,37              : ... to after 6

700 DATA 12,37,13,35,14,33              : ... to after 7

710 DATA 11,38,12,33,13,28              : ... to after 8

720 DATA 11,38,10,33,9,28               : ... to after 9

730 DATA 10,38,9,36,8,34                : ... to after 10

740 DATA 10,38,8,37,6,36                : ... to after 11

750 DATA 10,40,8,41,6,42                : ... to after 12

800 GOSUB 2000                          : Clear screen

810 X=8 : Y=30 : GOSUB 2100             : Position cursor

820 PRINT "THE CLOCK GAME"              :

830 X=15 : Y=10 : GOSUB 2100            :

840 RANDOMIZE                           : See general note 1

850 X=20 : Y=1 : GOSUB 2100             :

860 INPUT "SKILL LEVEL (1=Hr  2=1/2 Hr  3=  : Enter level of skill
    1/4 Hr  4=All): ",LEVEL$            :

1000 GOSUB 2000                         : Clear screen

1005 IF LEVEL$="1" THEN BIG=12          : Hours only; BIG is the position

                                        :    of the big hand

1010 IF LEVEL$="2" THEN BIG=6*(INT(RND*2)+1): Hours or half hours only

1020 IF LEVEL$="3" THEN BIG=3*(INT(RND*4)+1): Hours, half hours or quarter

                                        :    hours

1030 IF LEVEL$="4" THEN BIG=INT(12*RND+1)  : 5-minute intervals

1040 LIT=INT(12*RND+1)                  : LIT is the hour (random 1-12)

1050 IF LIT=BIG THEN GOTO 1005          : Overlapped hands are confusing

1060 'Draw the clock face               :
```

```
1070 X=11 : Y=39 : GOSUB 2100              ¦

1080 PRINT "+"                             ¦ Clock center

1120 FOR AA=1 TO 12                        ¦ Loop to

1130    X=XFACE(AA) : Y=YFACE(AA)-1        ¦ Y term contains -1 because the

1140    GOSUB 2100                         ¦    PRINT prints " 1", etc

1150    PRINT AA                           ¦

1160 NEXT AA                               ¦

1170 FOR AA=1 TO NPBIG(BIG)                ¦ Loop to draw big hand points

1180    X=XBIG(BIG,AA) : Y=YBIG(BIG,AA)    ¦

1190    GOSUB 2100                         ¦

1200    PRINT "t"                          ¦

1210 NEXT AA                               ¦

1220 IF BIG > 6 AND BIG <> 12 THEN GOTO 1310¦ If the big hand is on 7-11, put

                                           ¦    little hand between numbers

1230 CC=4                                  ¦ This sequence for making little

                                           ¦    hands from shortened big hand

1240 IF LIT=2 OR LIT=4 OR LIT=8 OR LIT=10  ¦ CC is number of big hand points
     THEN CC=3                             ¦    used

1250 FOR AA=1 TO CC                        ¦ Loop to draw little hand

1260    X=XBIG(LIT,AA) : Y=YBIG(LIT,AA)    ¦

1270    GOSUB 2100                         ¦

1280    PRINT "t"                          ¦

1290 NEXT AA                               ¦

1300 GOTO 1400                             ¦ Go around next sequence

1330 FOR AA=1 TO 3                         ¦ Begin sequence to draw little
```

```
1340    X=XLITOF(LIT,AA) : Y=YLITOF(LIT,AA) :     hand between numbers

1350    GOSUB 2100                          :

1360    PRINT "!";                          :

1370 NEXT AA                                :

1400 X=4 : Y=60 : GOSUB 2100               : Display # right/# tries

1410 PRINT RIGHT;"/";TRIES                  :

1500 X=21 : Y=30 : GOSUB 2100              :

1510 INPUT "WHAT TIME IS IT? ",HR,MIN       : Input time; the hours and

                                            :    minutes are separated by a

                                            :    comma; your computer may

                                            :    allow a formatted input so a

                                            :    colon may be used

1530 IF MIN=0 THEN MIN=60                   : Adjust for even hour

1540 IF HR=LIT AND MIN=BIG!5 THEN           : Test answer

     GOTO 3000 ELSE GOTO 3500               :

1999 '=========================             :

2000 'Subroutine to clear screen            :

2010 '=========================             :

2020 PRINT CHR$(26)                         :

2030 RETURN                                 :

2099 '===================================  :

2100 'Subroutine to position cursor at X,Y :

2101 '===================================  :

2110 PRINT CHR$(27);"=";CHR$(32+X);         :

     CHR$(32+Y);                            :
```

```
2120 RETURN                          !

2999 '===============================  !

3000 'Subroutine to reward right answer  !

3001 '===============================  !

3010 X=11 : Y=38                      !

3020 FOR AA=1 TO 3                    !

3030    PRINT CHR$(7)                 ! Ring bell

3040    GOSUB 2100                    ! Print "YES" 3 times

3050    PRINT "YES"                   !

3060    FOR BB=1 TO 400 : NEXT BB     !

3065 GOSUB 2100                       !

3070    PRINT "    "                  ! Print blank

3080    FOR BB=1 TO 400 : NEXT BB     !

3090 NEXT AA                          !

3110 RIGHT=RIGHT+1 : TRIES=TRIES+1    ! Increment # right, # of tries

3120 GOTO 1000                        ! Try another one (infinite loop)

3500 '===========================     !

3501 'Subroutine for wrong answer     !

3502 '===========================     !

3510 X=11 : Y=38 : GOSUB 2100         !

3520 PRINT "NO!"                      !

3530 TRIES=TRIES+1                    ! Increment # tries

3540 X=21 : Y=46 : GOSUB 2100         !

3550 PRINT "         "                ! Erase previous try

3560 X=21 : Y=15 : GOSUB 2100         !
```

```
3570 PRINT "TRY AGAIN!"                    :

3580 GOTO 1400                             :

4000 END
```

The Spelling Game

This game is designed to teach spelling of simple words of your choice in a step-by-step manner. The word is presented on the screen; then the child must either fill in missing letters from the word, or spell the whole word, or both, as desired. The game is set up for twenty words of up to four letters each. However, it is easily adapted to any number of words of any length. It is suggested that you start with a few words and build up the "dictionary" gradually.

```
1 ' The Spelling Game                      :

2 ' !!!!!!!!!!!!!!!!!!!                                :

10 GOSUB 1000                              : Clear screen

20 X=10 : Y=32 : GOSUB 1100                : Position cursor

30 PRINT "The Spelling Game"               :

40 X=15 : Y=20 : GOSUB 1100                :

50 RANDOMIZE                               : See general note 1

60 X=20 : Y=10 : GOSUB 1100                :

70 INPUT "Enter skill level (1=single      : Fill in the missing letter or
   letter, 2=whole word, 3=both): ",LEVEL  :    spell the whole word or both

80 DIM WORD$(20,4) , NLET(20)              : 20 words of at most 4 letters--
                                           :    you may use more or bigger
                                           :    words

90 FOR AA=1 TO 20                          : Loop to read words
```

```
100    READ NLET(AA)                        !  Number of letters in word

110    FOR BB=1 TO NLET(AA)                  !  Read each letter of the word as

120      READ WORD$(AA,BB)                   !      a separate array element

130    NEXT BB                              !

140 NEXT AA                                 !

499 ' The play begins here                 !

500 NWORD = INT (RND#19.5 + 1)              !  Choose a random word 1-20

510 IF NWORD=D1 OR NWORD=D3 THEN 500        !  Don't use same word as last

                                            !      time or the time before

520 D2=D1 : D1=NWORD                        !  Reset last 2 word values

530 GOSUB 1000 : GOSUB 1200                 !  Clear screen; display score

540 X=10 : Y=37 : GOSUB 1100                !

550 FOR AA=1 TO NLET(NWORD)                 !  Loop to display word

560    PRINT WORD$(NWORD,AA);" ";           !

570 NEXT AA                                 !

580 X=18 : Y=25 : GOSUB 1100                !

590 INPUT "Read the word and hit RETURN",   !

    DUMMY$                                  !

600 IF LEVEL=2 THEN 760                     !  If spell whole word only, skip

610 FOR AA=NLET(NWORD) TO 1 STEP -1         !  Loop to display word with 1

620    GOSUB 1000 : GOSUB 1200              !      missing letter at a time

630    X=10 : Y=36 : GOSUB 1100             !

640    FOR BB=1 TO NLET(NWORD)              !  Loop to display word letters

650      IF AA=BB THEN PRINT "_ "; ELSE     !  Missing letter

         PRINT WORD$(NWORD,BB);" ";         !
```

```
660    NEXT BB                           !

670    X=15 : Y=27 : GOSUB 1100          !

680    PRINT "Enter the missing letter"  !

690    GOSUB 1200                        !

700    GUESS$ =INPUT$(1)                 ! Input missing letter (see

                                         !   general note 2)

710    X=10 : Y=36+2*(AA-1) : GOSUB 1100 ! Position to print GUESS$ in

720    PRINT GUESS$                      !   place of the missing letter

730    FOR CC=1 TO 500 : NEXT CC         ! Wait

740    IF GUESS$ = WORD$(NWORD,AA) THEN  ! Test GUESS$

       GOSUB 2000 ELSE GOSUB 3000 : GOTO 690!

750 NEXT AA                              !

760 IF LEVEL = 1 THEN 500                ! If missing letter only, skip

770 GOSUB 1000                           !

780 X=10 : Y=32 : GOSUB 1100             !

790 PRINT "Spell the word"               !

800 X=15 : Y=36 : GOSUB 1100             !

810 FOR AA=1 TO NLET(NWORD)              ! Loop to print "_" to represent

820    PRINT "_ ";                       !   word letters

830 NEXT AA                              !

840 FOR AA=1 TO NLET(NWORD)              ! Loop to input word letters

850    GOSUB 1200                        !

860    X=15 : Y= 36 + (AA-1)*2 : GOSUB 1100 ! Cursor to each letter position

870    GUESS$ = INPUT$(1)                !

880    PRINT GUESS$                      !
```

```
890    IF GUESS$ <> WORD$(NWORD,AA) THEN    : Test GUESS$

       GOSUB 3000 : GOTO 850               :

900    IF AA < NLET(NWORD) THEN RIGHT=      : Increment RIGHT and TRIES only

       RIGHT+1 : TRIES=TRIES+1             :    if not going to in 2000

910 NEXT AA                                 :

920 FOR DD=1 TO 400 : NEXT DD               : Wait

930 COUNT=NLET(NWORD) : GOSUB 2000          : Set count at final pass for this

940 GOTO 500                                :    word

1000 '=========================             :

1001 'Subroutine to clear screen            :

1002 '=========================             :

1010 PRINT CHR$(26)                         : Clear screen (general note 3)

1020 RETURN                                 :

1100 '===================================   :

1101 'Subroutine to position cursor at X,Y  :

1102 '===================================   :

1110 PRINT CHR$(27); "="; CHR$(32+X) ;      : Position cursor at line X,

     CHR$ (32+Y);                           :    column Y (general note 4)

1120 RETURN                                 :

1200 '=========================             :

1201 'Subroutine to display score           :

1202 '=========================             :

1210 X=22 : Y=2 : GOSUB 1100                 :

1220 PRINT RIGHT; "/" ; TRIES               : RIGHT= number right

1230 RETURN                                 : TRIES= number right + wrong
```

```
2000 '==================================== !

2001 'Subroutine to reward correct answer  !

2002 '==================================== !

2005 RIGHT=RIGHT+1 : TRIES=TRIES+1          ! Increment RIGHT, TRIES

2010 GOSUB 1000                             !

2020 X=10 : Y=36 : GOSUB 1100               !

2030 COUNT=COUNT+1                          ! Count letters to see if done

                                            !    with word

2040 FOR CC=1 TO NLET(NWORD)                ! Loop to spell out word slowly

2050   PRINT WORD$(NWORD,CC);" "; CHR$(7); ! Print each letter, ring bell

2060     FOR EE=1 TO 600 : NEXT EE          ! Wait

2070 NEXT CC                                !

2075 FOR DD=1 TO 300 : NEXT DD              ! Wait

2080 IF COUNT < NLET(NWORD) THEN RETURN     ! Don't do more unless word done

2085 IF COUNT=NLET(NWORD) AND               ! If going to spell whole word, do

     LEVEL<>1 THEN RETURN                   !    this before proceeding

2090 COUNT=0                                ! Reset COUNT after done with word

2100 GOSUB 1000                             !

2110 Y=37                                   !

2120 FOR X=2 TO 22 STEP 4                   ! Loop to print word many times

2130    GOSUB 1100                          !    when all done

2140       FOR CC=1 TO NLET(NWORD)          ! Loop to print each letter

2150          PRINT WORD$(NWORD,CC);" ";    !

2160       NEXT CC                          !

2180 NEXT X                                 !
```

```
2190 FOR CC=1 TO 1000 : NEXT CC         ! Wait

2200 RETURN                             !

3000 '===========================       !

3001 'Subroutine for wrong answer        !

3002 '===========================       !

3005 TRIES=TRIES+1                      ! Increment TRIES

3008 XTEMP=X : YTEMP=Y                  ! Save current values of X,Y

3010 X=21 : Y=32 : GOSUB 1100           !

3020 PRINT "NO! Try again." ; CHR$(7)   !

3030 X=XTEMP : Y=YTEMP : GOSUB 1100     !

3040 PRINT "_"                          ! Prepare for another try

3050 RETURN                             !

4000 DATA 3,A,N,D                       ! # of letters followed by the

4010 DATA 3,B,A,D                       !    letters in each word

4020 DATA 3,C,A,T                       ! More or bigger words may be used

4030 DATA 3,D,O,G                       !    if the WORD$ array is

4040 DATA 3,E,L,F                       !    adjusted

4050 DATA 3,F,A,T                       !

4060 DATA 2,G,O                         !

4070 DATA 3,H,O,P                       !

4080 DATA 2,I,T                         !

4090 DATA 3,J,A,M                       !

4100 DATA 4,L,A,M,B                     !

4110 DATA 3,M,A,N                       !

4120 DATA 3,N,O,T                       !
```

```
4130 DATA 3,P,I,6              :
4140 DATA 3,R,E,D              :
4150 DATA 3,S,A,D              :
4160 DATA 2,U,P                :
4170 DATA 3,T,O,P              :
4180 DATA 4,W,A,L,L            :
4190 DATA 3,V,A,N              :
5000 END                       :
```

The Adding Game

While the following game is designed for teaching pre-school children to add simple integers, it can easily be expanded to addition, subtraction, multiplication, and division of any numbers. The short, simple logic provides an ideal opportunity for you to be really creative in embellishing the graphics for right and wrong answers. If you're ambitious, you may want to present the numbers to be added in large format using the subroutines and data from "The Remember Game."

```
1 ' THE ADDING GAME              :
2 ' ################              :
10 PRINT CHR$(26)                : Clear screen
20 X=4 : Y=35 : GOSUB 1000       : Position cursor
30 PRINT "ADDING GAME"           :
40 X=12 : Y=30 : GOSUB 1000      :
50 INPUT " PRACTICE NUMBER = ", NUM  : The computer will ask for the sum
                                 :   of NUM and a random number
```

```
60 RANDOMIZE NUM                        !    between 0 and 9

70 PRINT CHR$(26)                       !

80 A = INT(RND#10)                      !  A is an integer 0 to 9

90 GOSUB 2000                           !  Display the score

100 X=12 : Y=33 : GOSUB 1000            !

110 PRINT NUM ; " + " ; A ; " = " ;     !  Present the addition problem

120  INPUT " " , SUM                    !  SUM is the player's answer

130 IF SUM=NUM+A THEN GOSUB 3000 ELSE   !  Test the answer

GOSUB 4000                              !

1000 '==============================    !

1001 ' Subroutine to position cursor    !

1002 '==============================    !

1010 PRINT CHR$(27);"=": CHR$(32+X);CHR$(32   !  Position cursor at line X, column Y

+Y);                                    !

1020 RETURN                             !

2000 '============================      !

2001 ' Subroutine to display score      !

2002 '============================      !

2010 X=2 : Y=2 : GOSUB 1000             !

2020 PRINT  RIGHT; " / " ; TRIES        !  RIGHT is number of right answers

                                        !  TRIES is total number of tries

2030 RETURN                             !

3000 '==============================    !

3001 'Subroutine for correct answer     !

3002 '==============================    !
```

```
3010 TRIES = TRIES + 1                    !  Increment TRIES

3020 RIGHT = RIGHT + 1                    !  Increment RIGHT

3030 X=18 : Y=33 : GOSUB 1000             !

3040 PRINT "                        "     !  Clear the line

3050 GOSUB 1000                           !

3060 PRINT "     Y E S" ; CHR$(7)         !

3070 FOR N=1 TO 2000 : NEXT N             !  Wait

3080 GOTO 70                              !  Do another

4000 '===========================        !

4001 'Subroutine for wrong answer         !

4002 '===========================        !

4010 TRIES = TRIES + 1                    !  Increment TRIES

4020 X=18 : Y=33 : GOSUB 1000             !

4030 PRINT "NO!   TRY AGAIN"              !

4040 FOR N=1 TO 1000 : NEXT N             !  WAIT

4050 X=12 : Y=33 : GOSUB 1000             !

4060 PRINT "                   "          !  Erase previous try

4070 GOTO 90                              !  Try again
```

Foods

When children are allowed to help prepare food, many of their negative attitudes toward eating certain foods are eliminated. If a child scrapes the carrots, it's almost sure he'll eat them! Furthermore, helping with food preparation helps a child become independent and experience accomplishment. This chapter gives food preparation ideas using your own favorite recipes and gearing them for child participation. The other recipes refer back to learning activities in chapter 1.

You may wish to make more detailed lesson plans to cover each of the four basic food groups discussed in chapter 1. The following lesson plan on dairy foods is an example.

Concepts:

1. Milk comes from cows.
2. Cream comes from milk.
3. Cream can be changed by adding air or cold.
4. Butter comes from cream.
5. Cheese is made from milk.

Learning Activities:

1. Take your child to a dairy and watch the cows being milked. If you know a dairy farmer, perhaps he will let you and your child milk a cow by hand.

2. Buy some unpasteurized, unhomogenized milk from a dairy. Keep it in a glass jar so you can observe the cream separating and rising to the top.

3. Whip the cream or make ice cream.

4. Fill a jar about half full of heavy cream. (Have the cream at room temperature for best results.) Add a clean wooden bead to the jar of cream. Place the lid on tightly. Shake the jar until the cream turns to butter. Drain off the liquid. You can add a dash of salt to the butter if you wish.

5. If you live near a cheese factory, visit it to see how the different kinds of cheeses are made.

Another approach to teaching food preparation would be to portray a recipe in pictures and then help your child follow the recipe.

Breads

When you make bread or rolls, divide the dough into balls about the size of a baseball and let your preschooler pound each ball of dough with a wooden mallet for a couple of minutes. This will knead the dough.

Sesame Sticks

Roll out your favorite roll dough into long, thin sticks. Dip the sticks into ¼ cup of melted butter. Then place them in a baking pan and sprinkle them with sesame seeds. Bake at 375 degrees F. for 8 to 10 minutes or until golden brown.

Individual Rolls

Roll out bread dough and cut into three-inch circles, or use prepared roll-dough rounds that are flattened. Butter the rolls and then let your child choose toppings for them.

Some possible toppings are shredded cheese, sesame seeds, brown sugar, cinnamon and sugar (mixed), raisins, chopped nuts. Bake until done.

Initial Pancakes

Use your favorite pancake-batter recipe. When the skillet is hot, pour batter to form your child's initial *backwards*. Cook until browned. Pour batter over the initial to form a pancake. Cook as usual, then flip. The initial will come out darker than the pancake. You can also use the numeral for your child's age.

Sweet-Roll Christmas Tree

Using your favorite sweet-roll recipe, arrange the rolls in the shape of a Christmas tree on a greased cookie sheet. Brush the rolls with melted butter. Sprinkle with brown sugar, nuts, and raisins. Bake according to the recipe. After baking, you can drizzle the tree with a powdered-sugar icing.

Popped Wheat

Place a thin layer of wheat in a baking dish. Sprinkle with two or three tablespoons of water. Season with salt, garlic salt, or onion salt. Bake at 400 degrees F. until the wheat's color changes to golden. Stir often. (The wheat will not pop open like popcorn.)

Fruits and Vegetables

Stuffed Celery

Clean and trim celery. Stuff it with peanut butter or soft cheese.

Carrot Curls

Clean carrots. Use a vegetable scraper to make long thin strips of carrots. Wrap these strips around your finger and secure with a toothpick. Place in a bowl of cold water and chill in the refrigerator for a couple of hours. Remove the toothpicks to serve.

Potato Crisps

Peel potatoes. Use a vegetable scraper to make long thin strips. Rinse the strips to remove the starch. Pat dry with paper towels. Fry the strips in hot oil. (Only Mom or Dad should work with the hot oil.) Drain on paper towels. Sprinkle with salt.

Potato Chips

Peel potatoes. Wash. Slice into thin rounds. Fry in hot oil. Drain on paper towels. Sprinkle with salt.

Marilyn's Leprechaun Soup

4 tablespoons butter
½ cup chopped onion
2 cups raw chopped potatoes, peeled
1¼ cup water
1½ teaspoon salt
⅛ teaspoon white pepper
10 oz. frozen chopped spinach
1 cup light cream
2 cups milk

Melt butter in a large saucepan. Sauté onion until golden. Add raw potatoes, water, salt, and pepper. Cover and simmer until potatoes are soft (about 30 minutes). Cook spinach and drain. Blend potatoes and spinach in the blender. Return to pan. Add milk and cream. Bring to a boil.

Toasted Pumpkin Seeds

Wash seeds thoroughly. Heat 2 tablespoons butter or oil in a frying pan. Stir in the clean seeds, coating them with the oil. Cook and stir until the seeds turn a golden brown. Spoon the seeds onto paper toweling and salt them lightly.

Variation: Add ½ teaspoon Worchestershire sauce to the butter for extra flavor (omit the salt).

Punkin Puddin'

1 package (3¾ oz.) instant vanilla pudding
½ cup pumpkin-pie filling (or you may use canned pumpkin and add your own spices)
1 ½ cups milk

Beat all ingredients together until thickened. Serve with whipped cream.

This recipe is also great for pumpkin tarts or pumpkin pie, using a graham-cracker crust.

Banana Sandwich

Replace the jelly or honey on your peanut-butter sandwich with slices of banana. You may also want to try apple slices or raisins with peanut butter.

Apple Turkeys

Lay an apple on its side. Place five toothpicks along the top of the wide part of the apple to form the turkey's tail. Place several raisins on each of the toothpicks for feathers. Use one toothpick with a corn candy or small gumdrop to form the head. You can place pieces of toothpicks under the turkey to form legs and provide balance.

Baked Apples

Wash and core baking apples. Place the apples in a baking dish. To each apple add 2 tablespoons brown sugar, 1 teaspoon butter, and a dash of cinnamon. Add enough water to cover the bottom of the baking dish. Bake at 375 degrees F. for about ½ hour or until the apples are tender. Serve hot with cream or ice cream.

Banana Shake

Blend together: 1 cup cold milk
1 banana
1 scoop vanilla ice cream

Meats

Meatballs

When making your favorite meatballs, let your child squeeze all of the ingredients together (with very clean hands) until they are well mixed. Then let him help you roll the mixture into balls.

Pizza

There are several easy things you can use for a pizza crust. Our favorites are fresh french bread cut lengthwise, or English muffins. You could also use canned biscuit dough and let your child roll out his own crust. Have all of the ingredients in individual bowls: spaghetti sauce, browned ground beef or Italian sausage, mushrooms, green pepper, olives, grated cheese—anything you like.

Let your child build his own pizza with the ingredients he wants. Bake in a pre-heated oven (450 degrees F.) until cheese is melted and pizza is heated through.

American Tacos

Have all of the following ingredients in separate bowls and "build" your own taco on your plate.

Corn chips

Ground beef, browned and seasoned with a small can of green chile salsa

Grated cheddar cheese

Shredded lettuce

Tomatoes, cubed

Sour cream

Wiener Boats

Slice wiener lengthwise just to the outer skin. Fold open and fill with mashed potatoes. Sprinkle potatoes with grated cheddar cheese. Bake at 350 degrees F. until heated through.

Wiener Wraps

Slice wiener lengthwise just to the outer skin. Fold open and place a slice of cheddar cheese inside. Wrap a slice of bacon around the wiener and secure with toothpicks. Place under broiler until bacon is cooked.

Individual Meat Pies

Use your favorite pie-crust recipe. Let your child roll out his own crust and place it into an individual-size pie tin. Fill the bottom with cubed chicken or turkey. Spoon on frozen or fresh mixed vegetables (cubed). Top with the following sauce:

Melt 2 tablespoons butter in a saucepan. Remove from heat and stir in 2 tablespoons flour. Salt and pepper to taste. When the flour is blended and smooth, return the pan to the flame and add ½ cup milk and ½ cup chicken broth. Stir constantly and bring to a boil. Cover pie with pastry, prick, and bake at 425 degrees F. for 30 minutes or until pastry is browned.

Eggs in a Boat

Cut a circle (about 2½ inches in diameter) in the center of a slice of bread. Butter one side of the bread. Toast the bread in a frying pan, buttered side down. Butter the top side; flip the toast when golden brown. Crack an egg into the center of the toast and continue cooking. Season to taste.

Treats

Nanny's Peek-a-Boo Cupcakes

Make your favorite cupcakes. After baking, cut a circle about an inch in diameter in the center of each cupcake and lift out the center of cake. Fill the hole with your favorite pudding and replace the cake center. (We like yellow cake with lemon pudding and butter cake with chocolate pudding.) Sprinkle the top with powdered sugar.

S'mores

Place a thin chocolate bar and hot roasted marshmallows between two graham crackers, or replace the graham crackers with apple slices.

Finger Jell-o

3 cups water
½ cup sugar
2 large packages flavored gelatin
5 envelopes un-flavored gelatin
2 cups cold water.

Bring 3 cups of water to a boil. Stir in the sugar and flavored gelatin until dissolved. In a separate bowl, mix 2 cups cold water with 5 envelopes of unflavored gelatin. Let sit for 15 minutes to dissolve. Combine the two mixtures. Pour onto a jelly-roll pan or other large flat pan with sides. Place in the refrigerator to cool. Cut into any shape desired, or use cookie cutters.

Jell-o Eggs

Blow out eggs, rinse the inside of the shells, and allow to dry.

Add one cup boiling water to a 3-oz. package of jello. When the jello is dissolved, add ½ cup cold water. Place the blown eggs in an empty egg carton with the large hole at the top. Fill the eggs with the Jell-o mixture and chill overnight. Gently crack and remove the shell. Serve on a bed of shredded lettuce. You may decorate the eggs with softened cream cheese using cake decorator tips.

Gingerbread Houses

Break graham crackers in half to form squares. Four squares will be used for the walls of the house, two more for the roof. "Glue" the crackers into place onto individual-sized milk cartons with royal frosting (recipe follows). Use more royal frosting for snow and to attach candies to the house. Build a snowman in the yard with marshmallows. Christmas trees can be made out of ice-cream cones, bushes from spearmint leaves, and so on.

Royal Frosting

4 egg whites
½ teaspoon cream of tartar
5 cups powdered sugar

Beat the egg whites with the cream of tartar until they are foamy. Slowly beat in the powdered sugar. Continue beating until the frosting is glossy (it will look like marshmallow cream) and will form a trench when cut through with a knife. Keep in an air-tight container until you are ready to use it.

Pretty Party Corn

Pop corn. Lightly butter and sprinkle with Jell-o powder.

Bar-B-Que Popcorn

Pop corn. Lightly butter and sprinkle with dry onion soup mix.

Cheese Corn

Pop corn. Lightly butter and sprinkle with Parmesan cheese or cheddar cheese powder.

Ghost Lollipops

Cover a lollipop with a square of white fabric tied at the "neck" with black yarn or shoe-string licorice. Color on big black eyes.

Arts and Crafts

There is a difference between arts and crafts. Gluing Popsicle sticks together to build a house is fun, and it teaches concentration and coordination, but it is not necessarily a creative art. It is a craft. A crafts project usually follows a standard pattern and uses certain standard materials.

Art, on the other hand, does not have any limitations as to what materials are used or what the outcome of the project will be. The design is supplied by the artist. And, the finished product is often not as important as the experience gained in the process of creating.

Arts and crafts each give the child different experiences and fulfill different needs. It is important to give your child opportunities for both.

Some supplies to keep on hand for your arts and crafts projects are:

Stacks of scratch paper

Newsprint roll ends. These can be obtained (usually free) from any newspaper printer. They can be used for large coloring and painting projects.

Colored construction paper

Large (about one inch wide) paintbrushes with long handles

Water-based paints

Finger paints

Water-based colored markers

Crayons

Child-sized (good quality) scissors
Cutting bag (described below)
Glue (in a dispenser bottle)
Playdough (recipe follows)
Child-sized rolling pins
Cookie cutters
Collage grab-bag (described below)
Beads and cord for stringing

Clay and Playdough Modeling

The value of molding playdough or clay includes sensory experience, self-expression, manipulation, emotional release, imagination, insight into one's own feelings, experimentation with form, and stimulation of thought.

Nancy's Perfect Playdough

1 cup water
2 teaspoons cream of tartar
½ cup salt
1 cup flour
1 tablespoon salad oil
A few drops of food coloring

Combine the ingredients in a saucepan and cook over medium heat (no hotter), stirring constantly until the mixture becomes very thick and pulls away from the sides of the pan. This usually takes only two or three minutes. Knead on the countertop until smooth. Keeps indefinitely in an airtight container.

Inedible Modeling Clay

2 cups flour
2 cups salt
½ cup (or more) hot water
1 tablespoon powdered alum

Mix the ingredients. Then add a teaspoon of cooking oil and some food coloring. When modeling, work on wax paper. Let the creations dry for several days or put them in a 250-degree oven for about three hours.

Edible Modeling Clay

Sprinkle a package of dry yeast into 1 ½ cups very warm water. Stir until the yeast is dissolved.
Mix: 1 egg
    ¼ cup honey
    ¼ cup shortening
    1 teaspoon salt
Add this to the yeast mixture

Stir in flour a little at a time until you have a ball of dough that's not too sticky to handle (about 5 cups).

Make flat figures on a cookie sheet. Cover the figures with a towel and let them rise for about 25 minutes. Bake for 20 minutes at 350 degrees. If you're not going to eat the figures, you can shellac them to preserve them.

Finger Painting

The value of finger painting includes sensory experience, satisfaction and enjoyment, self-expression, emotional release, insight into one's own feelings, and good work habits.

Finger Paint (No. 1)

1 cup liquid starch
6 cups water
½ cup soap flakes

Dissolve soap in water until smooth. Mix with starch and remaining water.

Finger Paint (No. 2)

Dissolve 12 tablespoons of starch in cold water. Add the mixture to two quarts of boiling water. Stir until thick. Pour into containers and add coloring. Add a few drops of oil of clove to preserve the colors. Store in a cool place.

To add variety to the texture of finger paints add salt and flour mixed with water or cornstarch mixed with water.

Our favorite finger paint is instant pudding or Danish dessert.

Painting

The values of painting include manipulation, learning good work habits, and small muscle development.
(Note: Add a small amount of liquid soap to your paints to help with cleanup.)

Bubble Painting

1 cup liquid soap
1 cup water
dry paint
Blow into the paint mixture with a straw until bubbles rise above the bowl. Place paper on top of the bubbles. The image of the bubbles will be "painted" on the paper.

Blow Painting

Mix dry paint with water to be quite thin. Put a spoonful of paint on the paper. Have your child blow through a straw to spread the paint around the paper.

Foot and Hand Painting

Make your paint moderately thick. Let your child walk through the paint and onto a long strip of paper. He can also dip his hands into the paint and make designs with them.

Spatter Painting

Make very thin paint. Cover a large area on the side of your house or a fence with paper. Let your child fling his paintbrush to make paint spatter onto the paper.

Water Painting

Let your child "paint" your house, sidewalk, and steps with a paintbrush and plain water. He can also use the spatter painting technique described above with water. Children really enjoy watching their creations disappear.

Sponge Painting

Clip a small piece of a sponge with a clothespin. Have your child dip the sponge in paint and then on the paper. You can also provide shapes cut out of stiff plastic to sponge around to make silhouettes.

String Painting

Fold construction paper in half. Dip yarn into thin paint. Arrange the yarn inside the folded paper. Press down on top of the paper while pulling out the yarn.

Salt Painting

Mix salt with dry tempura paint. Put this mixture into salt shakers. "Paint" a design on the paper with glue, and sprinkle the colored salt onto the glue.

Papier Mâché

The value of papier mâché includes sensory experience, emotional release, manipulation, imagination, and self-expression.

Mix wheat paste or wallpaper paste into warm water

until you have a thin, creamy paste. Or, mix ⅓ cup flour to ¼ cup water to make paste.

First, obtain objects on which to form your papier mâché. You might try balloons (pop the balloon and remove it after the sculpture has dried), bottles, rolled paper, foil formed into any shape, and cardboard tubes.

Then dip paper strips (about one inch wide torn from newspapers) in the paste and apply them to your form. Overlap the strips as you put them on.

Cover the base with two or three layers of strips.

Smooth the surface with your hand and wipe off any extra paste. Set your creation on waxed paper and let it dry completely.

Paint or decorate your sculpture when it is completely dry.

Collages

The value of collages includes self-expression, sensory experience, enjoyment, use of imagination, learning initiative, developing good work habits and eye-hand coordination, emotional release, manipulation, and exploration.

A collage is a picture made by pasting many different objects together on paper. Anything that can be glued on paper can be a part of your collage. You might try toothpicks, pipe cleaners, colored paper cut into shapes, yarn, lace, ribbon, beans, rice, buttons, cotton balls, leaves, sticks, flowers, egg-carton cups, seeds, doilies, colored salt, soap flakes, rubber bands, and straws.

Go on a walk with your child and collect objects from nature: sticks, leaves, flowers, seeds, grass, sand, and so on. When you get home, your child can make a collage out of his collection.

Have on hand a grab-bag to which you continually add items of different textures, sizes, and shapes from which your child can choose to make a collage.

Cutting and Pasting

The value of cutting and pasting includes developing good work habits, skill and concentration, eye-hand coordination, and small-muscle development.

Cut colored tissue paper into many shapes and sizes. Using a paintbrush, glue these shapes onto white construction paper with liquid starch, overlapping the tissue paper. This will create a stained-glass effect. (Overlapping yellow on blue will make green, and so on.)

Provide a cutting bag for your child. In it put a pair of good quality children's scissors, colorful ads and junk mail, or any other colorful paper to cut up.

Miscellaneous

Thumbprint Pictures

Using an ink pad, make fingerprints on paper. Then use pens or crayons to fill in features on the prints to create people, animals, flowers, and so on.

Melted Crayon Pictures

Scrape crayons with a vegetable scraper. Arrange the crayon pieces on waxed paper. Fold the waxed paper in half, covering the crayon shavings. Place one brown paper bag under and one over the waxed paper and press with a warm iron. Place the finished picture on black construction paper for a frame.

Vegetable Printing

Cut a raw vegetable (potato, carrot, turnip) so that you have a flat surface. Carve a design in the surface with the shape you desire higher than the rest of the vegetable. Dip your design into paint and stamp it onto paper. (Because a sharp knife must be used for this, cutting and carving of the vegetable must be done by an adult.) Vegetables like onions, broccoli, and cauliflower may also be used for printing, without the need for cutting a design.

Life-sized Self-Portrait

Have your child lie down on a large piece of newsprint paper. Trace around his entire body with a colored marker. With colored markers or crayons, let your child fill in his own features; face, hair, clothes, and so on.

Rubbings

Place any object under a sheet of paper. Using the side of a crayon that has had the paper removed, rub over the top of the paper. An image of the object under your paper will appear. Try leaves, seeds, flowers, coins, and other objects or textured surfaces or fabrics.

Physical Activities

Until I had three children and was living in a small apartment in the East, I didn't realize there was a need to provide special physical activities for children. I thought they got all of the exercise they needed naturally. Not so. Like adults, children need to work on exercising all of the muscles in their bodies. This chapter contains fun activities that will exercise and develop all parts of your child's body. These exercises also teach coordination and balance. Included are exercise programs for the balance beam and trampoline. Some of the following instructions are in italics. These you should read to your child while helping him follow them (as needed).

Warmups

1. *Sit on the floor with your legs crossed ("Indian style") and move your head from side to side, touching your ears to your shoulders. Next, move your head forward and back, touching your chin to your chest and then stretching your chin up to the sky.*
2. *Wiggle your fingers. Shake out both your hands. Roll your arms backward and then forward, making big circles.*
3. *Sit with your feet stretched out straight in front of you. Point and flex your feet. Wiggle your toes. Bend over and touch your nose to your knees.*

4. Still sitting, "walk" your fingers down your legs from your knees to your toes. Now tickle your toes!

5. While sitting on the floor, spread your feet apart. Touch your nose to your right knee, your left knee, and then the floor between your knees.

Exercises

Butterfly

Sit on the floor. Pull your feet up to your body, holding onto your ankles. Flap your knees up and down like the wings of a butterfly. Bend over and touch your nose to your toes.

Superman

Lie on your stomach with your arms stretched out over your head. Raise your hands, head, shoulders, and feet off the ground (to fly like superman!). Stay this way for a count of three, then relax.

Breast Stroke

Lie on the floor as you do for "Superman." When you rise up off the floor, swing your arms out and around to your sides as if you were swimming.

Make a Bridge

Lie on your back. Bring your hands over your head and then back to your ears. Push off the floor with your hands and feet to form an arch with your body.

Washing Machine

Stand with your feet slightly apart. Bring your arms straight out to your sides, even with your shoulders. Drop the lower part of your arm (from the elbow) so that your hands hang to your sides. Twist your body from the waist facing as far to the left as you can; then twist to the right in a "washer" action. When you start, push your belly button to start the machine.

Donkey Kicks

Begin in a standing position. Put both hands down on the floor in front of your feet. Kick both feet up behind you, balancing on your hands. (This is the beginning of learning handstands.)

Head Stands

Have your child put his head down on the floor about eight inches from the wall, facing away from the wall. Help him raise his feet and balance them against the wall. Soon he will be able to raise up against the wall by himself. This will teach him how to pull in his stomach muscles and balance to do a head stand away from the wall.

Animal Walks

Move around like many different animals. For example, walk on your hands and feet to be a spider (or bear); hop like a frog; crawl like a snake; swim like a fish; fly like a bird; waddle like a duck.

Wheelbarrow

Have your child lie on his stomach on the floor. Next, have him rise up on his hands while you lift his feet off the ground by holding onto his ankles. Have him walk around the house on his hands. When he gets stronger, let him try walking up the stairs!

Chop Wood

Stand with your feet apart. Clasp your hands over your head as if you were holding onto an ax. Swing your arms down as far behind you as you can (through your legs), then swing them back up to the starting position.

Head-to-Toe

Lie on your stomach. Push up off the floor with your hands, arching your back and bringing your feet up to touch your head. Hold the position until you count to five.

Statue Dance

Dance to music. When the music stops, you freeze. Continue dancing when the music starts again.

Row Your Boat

Sit on the floor facing your child. Both of you stretch out your legs in the straddle position. Touch your feet to your child's feet. Hold hands. Lean forward and back in a rowing motion as you sing the familiar tune "Row, Row, Row Your Boat."

Motorboat

This is better with three or more children (you can join in too). Stand in a circle holding hands. All move in the same direction, gradually gaining speed as you chant: "Motor boat, motor boat, go so slow. Motor boat, motor boat, go so fast. Motor boat, motor boat, step on the gas!"

Beanbag Toss

This is better with three or more children. Have the children sit in a large circle on a rug or carpet. Place a basket and one beanbag for each child in the center of the circle. Have each child in turn hop or skip to the center of the circle, pick up his beanbag, and hop back to his place. Then from his place he tosses the beanbag into the basket.

Miscellaneous

Hang balloons or crepe-paper streamers from the ceiling just out of your child's reach. Have him jump to reach them.

Have your child hop on one foot on a straight line, a zigzag line, and a circle that you have made on your floor with masking tape. Then have him change feet and try again.

Place two long pieces of yarn parallel to each other on the floor about two feet apart. Have your child "jump over the river." As he improves, widen the "river."

String a cord about six inches from the ground between two pegs. (The goal posts from your croquet set are perfect.) Have your child jump over and crawl under the cord.

Make "body position cards" by cutting a piece of poster board into about eight-by-eleven-inch pieces. On each card, draw one of the symbols below. (The starred symbols can be turned up-side-down when playing the game.) Hold up one card at a time and ask your child to "make his body look like the picture."

Exercises for the Balance Beam

Many educators believe that through the development of large muscles and the improvement of coordination resulting from regular exercise on the balance beam, reading ability is improved.

A balance beam can easily be made from a four-by-four-inch wooden beam about ten feet long. Sand it down to remove splinters and sharp corners. To stop the beam from rolling, attach to the bottom two cross bars made from one-by-four-inch pieces of wood about two feet long. Read the italicized instructions to your child and, as needed, help him follow them.

1. *Walk forward on the beam, arms held out to your sides for balance.*

2. *Walk sideways on the beam by moving one foot forward on the beam and then bringing the other foot forward to meet it.*

3. *Do a spider (or bear) walk: walk forward on the beam on your hands and feet.*

4. *Walk backward on the beam.*

5. *Do a spider walk backward.*

6. *Do a V sit. Sit on the beam in tuck position (knees brought up to chest, and feet flat on the beam). Put your hands behind you on the beam for balance. Raise your feet up, pointing your toes to form a V with your body.*

7. *Kneel on your hands and knees on the beam. Raise one leg up straight behind you. Hold and count to five. Repeat with the other leg.*

8. *Lie on your back on the beam with your hands stretched over your head and your knees up with your feet flat on the beam. With a swinging motion, bring your feet and your hands together balancing over the center of your body.*

9. *Lie on your back on the beam with your hands stretched over your head and your legs brought straight up so your body forms an L. Slowly let your feet drop down to your sides, forming a straddle. Bring your feet back together.*

10. *Do "Superman" on the beam [see page 144].*

11. *Stand on the beam with your arms out to your sides for balance. Raise one foot out in front of your body and off of the beam. Balance. Repeat with your other foot.*

12. *Stand on the beam with your arms out to your sides for balance. Raise up onto your toes. Hold your position and then come down.*

13. *Walk to the middle of the beam, turn around, and come back.*

14. Place several beanbags along the beam. *Step over the bags as you walk forward, backward, and sideways.*

15. *Hop with both feet on the beam.*

16. *Stand on the beam with your feet together. Close your eyes and see how high you can count and still stay on the beam.*

17. *Do the same as above, standing on one foot only. Repeat on the other foot.*

Trampoline Exercises

Jumping is wonderful exercise. Besides strengthening the muscles in the legs, it is a good aerobic exercise, working the heart and lungs. It is also good "therapy" for grumpy children. It's easy to work out frustration, anger, or boredom on a trampoline. (You might want to try it too!)

A good substitute for a trampoline is an old double-bed-sized box spring and mattress placed directly on the floor (no frame) and pushed up into a corner of the room. Read the italicized instructions to your child and, as needed, help him follow them.

Straight Jump

Get the feel of the trampoline with a basic up-and-down jump, bringing your feet together when you are up in the air. Experiment with arm movements: fly like a bird or make big circles with your arms.

Seat Drop

When you are up in the air, bring your feet straight forward and land on your seat using your hands for balance. Bounce back up and land on your feet.

Seat Drop, Spin

Do a seat drop as above, only instead of coming up on your feet, spin around to face backward and come down on your seat again.

Knee Drop

When you are up in the air, bring your feet back and land on your knees. Bounce back up and land on your feet.

Jump and Spin

When you are up in the air, turn around to face the opposite direction. Next, try turning around in a complete circle.

Straddle Jump

When you are up in the air, bring your feet out to your sides as if you were doing the splits.

Pike Jump

When you are up in the air, bring your knees up to touch your chest and slap them. When you come back down, land on your feet and bring your hands over your head.

Doggie Drop

Drop down onto all fours; then come back up onto your feet.

Books and Poetry

You've heard it before, and it's true: The best way to get your child to enjoy books is to enjoy them yourself. Let him see you reading books, and take time to read to him each day. Take regular trips to the library together and let your child choose some of the books he will take home. Your best resource is a good librarian. Get to know her and use her talents. Your child's attitude toward books and reading will influence his attitude toward school. An excellent resource for helping you choose your children's books is *The Read Aloud Handbook*, by Jim Trelease.

This chapter contains four book lists: Caldecott winners, Newbery winners, our own favorites, and poetry books.

The Caldecott Award is one of the best-known awards in children's literature. It began in 1938 and was named in honor of Randolf Caldecott, noted English illustrator of the nineteenth century. The award is given each year for excellence in illustration. These, then, are picture books, and are geared generally for the younger child, preschool to early grade school.

Because art preferences vary, you may find you do not care for some of these books. I am not necessarily recommending all of these books as favorites, but this is a good starting place to find out what you and your child do like.

The Caldecott Award Books

1985 *Saint George and the Dragon,* by Trina Schart Hyman

1984 *Shadow,* by Marcia Brown

1983 *Jumanji,* by Chris Van Allsburg

1982 *Fables,* by Arnold Lobel

1981 *The Oxcart Man,* by Donald Hall

1980 *The Girl Who Loved Wild Horses,* by Paul Goble

1979 *Noah's Ark,* by Peter Spier

1978 *Ashanti to Zulu,* by Margaret Musgrove

1977 *Why Mosquitoes Buzz in People's Ears,* by Verna Aardema

1976 *Arrow to the Sun,* by Gerald McDermott

1975 *Duffy and the Devil,* by Harve Zemach

1974 *The Funny Little Woman,* by Arlene Mosel

1973 *One Fine Day,* by Nonny Hogrogian

1972 *A Story, a Story,* by Gail E. Haley

1971 *Sylvester and the Magic Pebble,* by William Steig

1970 *The Fool of the World and the Flying Ship,* by Arthur Ransome

1969 *Drummer Hoff,* by Barbara Emberley

1968 *Sam, Bangs and Moonshine,* by Evaline Ness

1967 *Always Room for One More,* by Sorche Nic Leodhas

1966 *May I Bring a Friend?* by Beatrice Schenk De Regniers

1965 *Where the Wild Things Are,* by Maurice Sendak

1964 *The Snowy Day,* by Ezra Jack Keats

1963 *Once a Mouse . . . ,* by Marcia Brown

1962 *Baboushka and the Three Kings,* by Ruth Robbins

1961 *Nine Days to Christmas,* by Marie Hall Ets and Aurora Labastida

1960 *Chanticleer and the Fox,* by Geoffrey Chaucer

1959 *Time of Wonder,* by Robert McCloskey

1958 *A Tree is Nice,* by Janice Udry

1957 *Frog Went a-Courtin',* by John Langstaff

The Newbery Award began in 1922 and is awarded each year for excellence in writing children's literature. The award was named in honor of John Newbery of London, who in the eighteenth century was first to publish books specifically for children. These books are geared for grade-school aged children to adults.

The Newbery Award Books

1985   *The Hero and the Crown*, by Robin McKinley
1984   *Dicey's Song*, by Cynthia Voight
1983   *A Visit to William Blake's Inn*, by Nancy Willard
1982   *Jacob Have I Loved*, by Katherine Paterson
1981   *The Gathering of Days*, by Joan W. Blos
1980   *Westing Game*, by Ellen Raskin
1979   *Bridge to Terabithia*, by Katherine Paterson
1978   *Roll of Thunder, Hear My Cry*, by Mildred Taylor
1977   *The Grey King*, by Susan Cooper
1976   *M.C. Higgins, the Great*, by Virginia Hamilton
1975   *The Slave Dancer*, by Paula Fox
1974   *Julie of the Wolves*, by Jean Craighead George
1973   *Mrs. Frisby and the Rats of Nimh*, by Robert C. O'Brien
1972   *The Summer of the Swans*, by Betsy Byars
1971   *Sounder*, by William H. Armstrong
1970   *The High King*, by Lloyd Alexander
1969   *From the Mixed-up Files of Mrs. Basil E. Frankweiler*, by E. L. Konigsburg
1968   *Up a Road Slowly*, by Irene Hunt
1967   *I, Juan de Pareja*, by Elizabeth Borton de Trevino
1966   *Shadow of a Bull*, by Maia Wojciechowska
1965   *It's Like This, Cat*, by Emily Neville
1964   *A Wrinkle in Time*, by Madeleine L'Engle
1963   *The Bronze Bow*, by Elizabeth George Speare

1962 *Island of the Blue Dolphins*, by Scott O'Dell
1961 *Onion John*, by Joseph Krumgold
1960 *The Witch of Blackbird Pond*, by Elizabeth George
      Speare
1959 *Rifles for Watie*, by Harold Keith
1958 *Miracles on Maple Hill*, by Virginia Sorensen
1957 *Carry On, Mr. Bowditch*, by Jean Lee Latham

My Preschoolers' Favorites

Make Way for Ducklings, by Robert McCloskey
Stone Soup, by Marcia Brown
Caps for Sale, by Esphyr Slobodkina
Lyle, Lyle Crocodile, by Bernard Waber
Father Fox's Pennyrhymes, by Clyde Watson; illustrated by
Wendy Watson
Alexandra the Rock-Eater, by Dorothy Van Woerkom; illustrated by Rosekrans Hoffman
Crow Boy, by Taro Yashima
Noah's Ark, by Peter Spier
The Judge, by Harve Zemach; illustrated by Margot Zemach
Why Mosquitoes Buzz in People's Ears, by Verna Aardema;
illustrated by Leo and Diane Dillon
Gilberto and the Wind, by Marie Hall Ets
Mike Mulligan and His Steam Shovel, by Virginia Lee Burton
Sylvester and the Magic Pebble, by William Steig
Goodnight Moon, by Margaret Wise Brown
Anno's Alphabet, by Mitsumasa Anno
Anno's Counting Book, by Mitsumasa Anno
Frog and Toad Together, by Arnold Lobel (look for the entire
Frog and Toad series)
Aesop's Fables, illustrated by Heidi Holder
Where the Wild Things Are, by Maurice Sendak
Ed Emberley's A B C, by Ed Emberley
The Little Red Hen, by Paul Galdone

The Train, by David McPhail
The Tale of Peter Rabbit, by Beatrix Potter; illustrated by Allen Atkinson
The Lord Is My Shepherd, illustrated by Tasha Tudor
Rain, by Peter Spier
Strega Nona, by Tomie de Paola
Green Eggs and Ham, by Dr. Seuss
Bedtime for Frances, by Russell Hoban
The Carrot Seed, by Ruth Krauss
The Gingerbread Boy, by Paul Galdone
Professor Wormbog in Search for the Zipperump-a-Zoo, by Mercer Mayer
The Very Hungry Caterpillar, by Eric Carle

Poetry Books

An Arkful of Animals, by William Cole
A Child's Garden of Verses, by Robert Louis Stevenson
I Went to the Animal Fair, by William Cole
Egg Thoughts and Other Frances Songs, by Russell Hoban
Cats and Bats and Things with Wings, by Conrad Aiken
Mother Goose, the classic Volland edition, illustrated by Frederick Richardson
Come Follow Me, by Gyo Fujikawa
A Little Laughter, compiled by Kathrine Lone
The Nutcracker Suite and Other Innocent Verses, by Ogden Nash
Toucans Two and Other Poems, by Jack Prelutsky

Patterns

Life-Cycle-of-a-Butterfly Chart

Cut the leaves out of green construction paper, the branch out of brown construction paper, and the butterfly out of plain paper so your child can decorate it. Glue these onto a large piece of paper.

Have your child take a tiny piece of playdough and form it into an "egg" to be glued onto the first leaf. (Explain that the butterfly lays her eggs on leaves so that when the caterpillar comes out, it will be able to eat the leaves and grow.)

On the second leaf, glue on anything fuzzy that will look like a caterpillar. I like using a short length of craft chenille. (Explain that after the caterpillar grows big enough, it spins a cocoon and rests.)

Make a cocoon by elongating a cotton ball and gluing it onto the tree branch. (After about two weeks, the caterpillar chews its way out of the cocoon and emerges as a beautiful butterfly.)

Puppets

There are many ways to make puppets. If you are interested in making elaborate puppets, there are several books on how to do so. Look for them at your library.

Some very simple puppets that we like to use are made from "stick-ons" that have been attached to a paper ring that fits around your finger (finger puppets). If you enjoy drawing, you can draw your own figures, or you can have your child draw figures to make finger puppets. You can also attach your drawings or stick-ons to Popsicle sticks. These are tiny puppets and are especially fun to use with your child when you are reading poetry, doing fingerplays, or singing songs.

Flying Butterfly or Helicopter

Trace the pattern onto colored construction paper. Cut along all solid lines. Fold along dotted lines A and B, going backward so the flaps overlap. Staple closed. Fold along dotted line C so that the "wing" goes away from you. Fold along dotted line D so that the "wing" comes toward you.

If you are making a butterfly, punch a hole in the bottom of the base and attach a long piece of string or yarn. Holding onto the string, your child can run and the "butterfly" will fly behind him.

If you are making a helicopter, do not attach a string. Have your child climb to the top of his slide (or another high place) and drop the helicopter, base first. It will whirl as it floats to the ground.

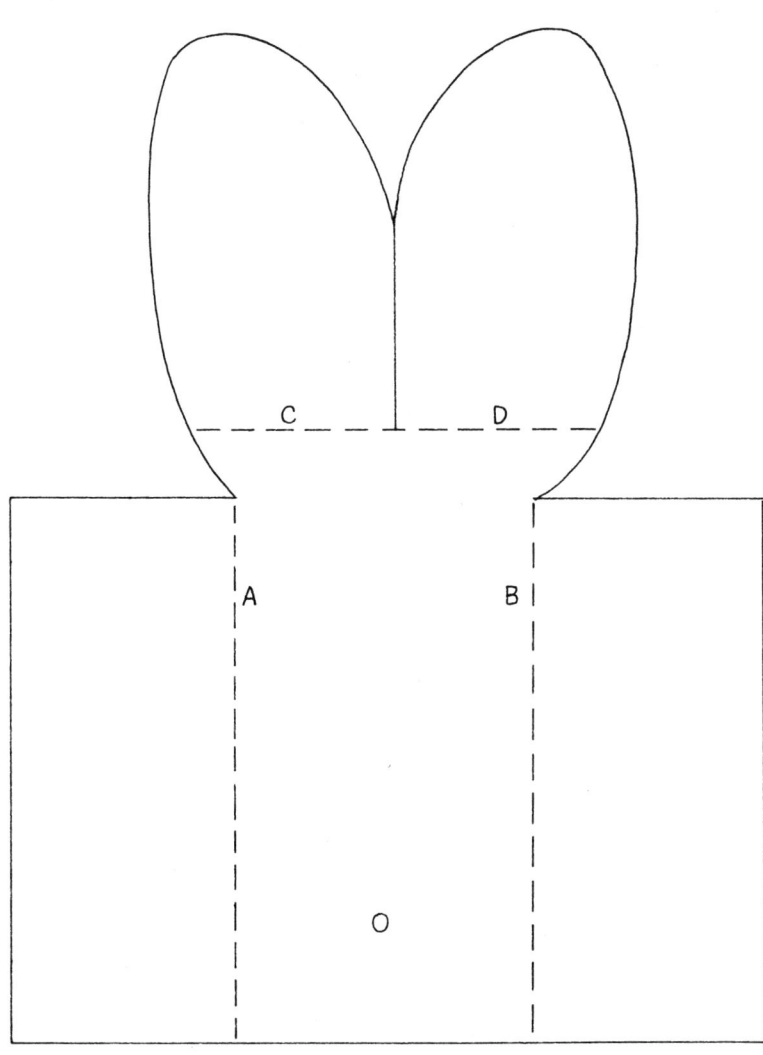

Paper Chains

Cut colored paper into strips about one inch wide and three to four inches long. Loop one strip to form a circle and staple it together. Thread a second strip through the first loop; loop it and secure it with a staple. Continue this process to make a chain as long as you wish.

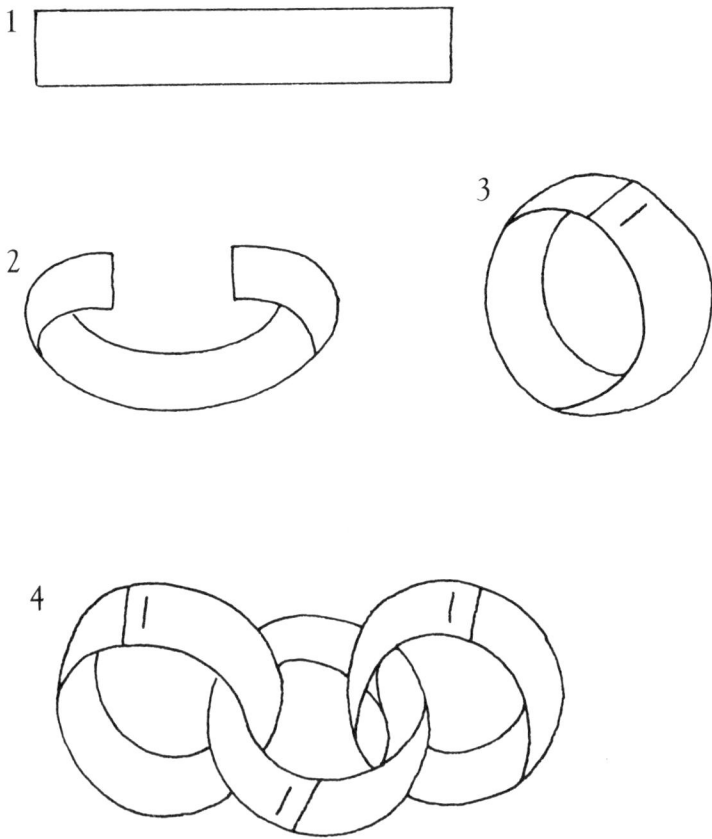

Shamrock

This shamrock pattern can be used during your lesson on Saint Patrick's Day (page 39) for home decorations and art projects with your child.

Teeth

These tooth patterns can be used in connection with your lesson on tooth care, page 19.

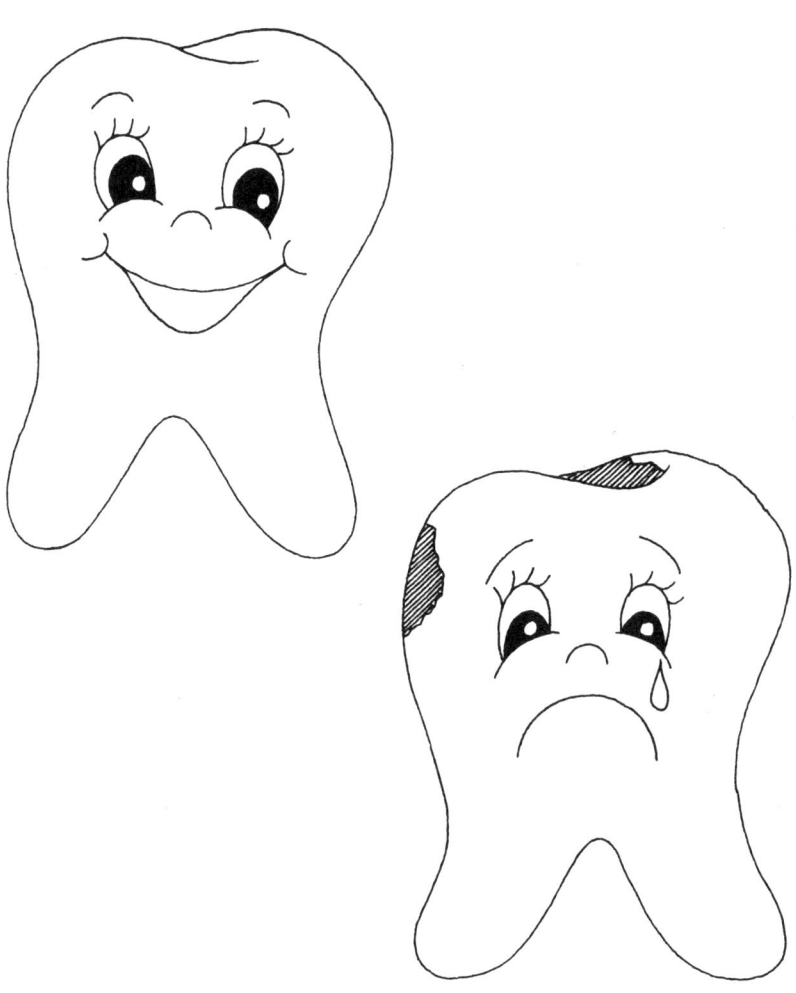

May Basket

Cut a large piece of colored paper into a square. Fold from corner to corner to form a triangle (figures 1 and 2). Next, fold A to D (figures 2 and 3), then B to C (figures 3 and 4). Now instead of folding the top edges down, fold the entire cup in half lengthwise (figures 4 and 5) and make a cut from the folded edge down to the "rim" of the cup (figure 5). Open the cup and fold down only the inside triangles made from the cut (figure 6). The edges remain for the handle of the basket.

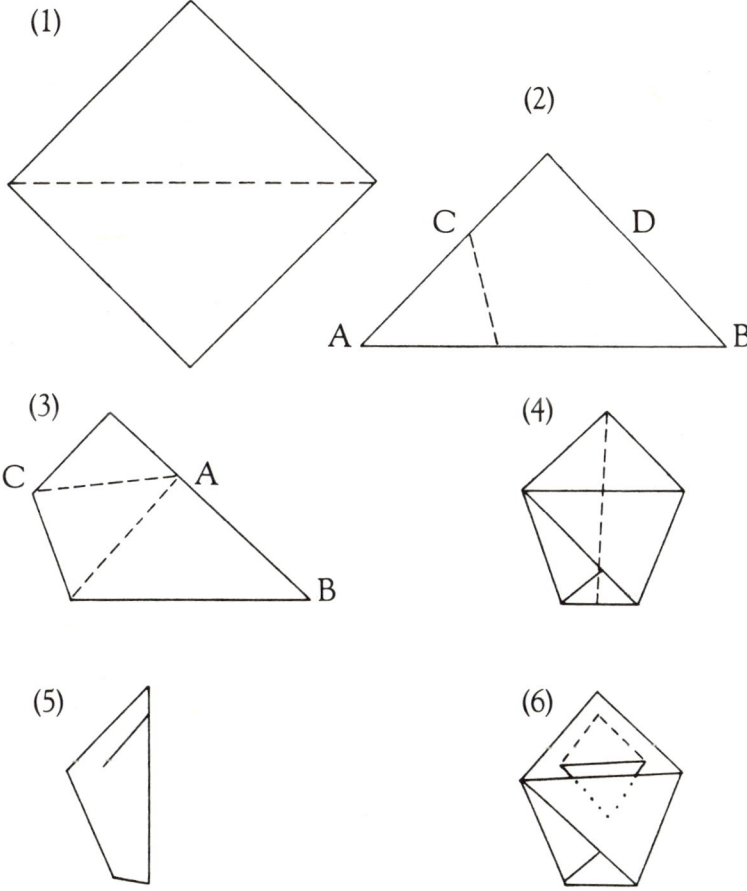

Birthday Crown

Cut out the crown from construction paper in your child's favorite color. Staple the band to the front piece at points A and B, adjusting the length to fit your child. Decorate.

Color Spinners

Cut out two circles about three inches in diameter, one each from red and yellow construction paper. Cut the yellow circle in half and glue half to the top and half to the underside of the red circle. Put a round toothpick through the center of the combined red and yellow circle. Spin it like a top. When it is spinning, it will appear to be orange. Try many combinations of colors.

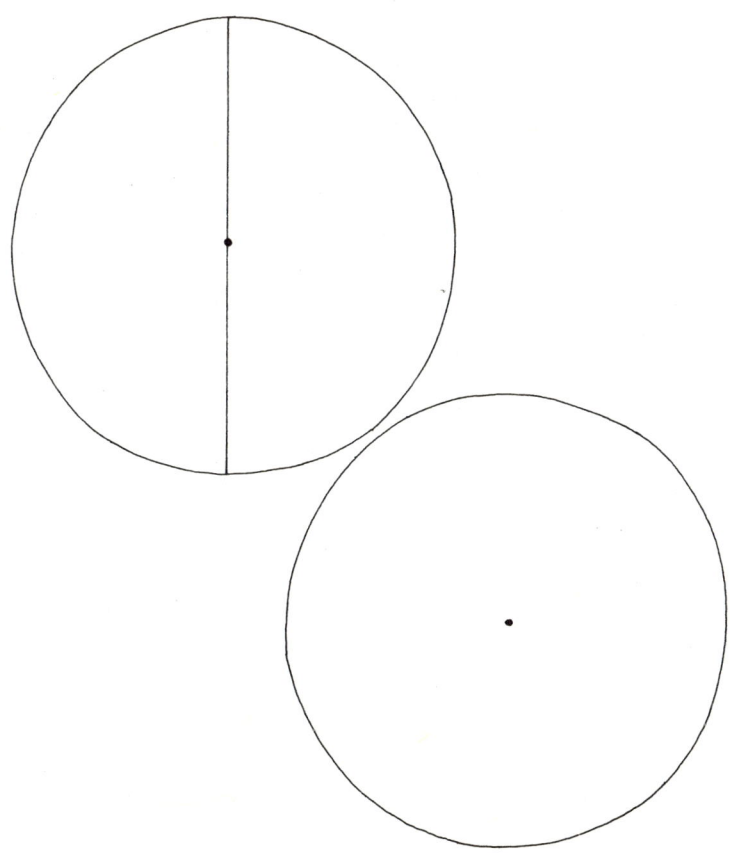

Three-Dimensional Zoo

Lay a small box (shoe boxes are good) on its side for a cage. Have your child draw pictures of animals to glue onto the back of the cage (bottom of the box), or you can put animal crackers or toy animals inside the cage. For bars, cut strips of construction paper cut about ¼ inch wide and long enough to cover the opening of your cage. Glue them to the box.

The *Mayflower*

Cut water out of blue construction paper, a boat out of brown, and a sail out of white. Punch two holes in the sail (as illustrated). Insert a straw cut about four inches long into the sail. Place the boat partially under the water. Glue all to a paper plate.

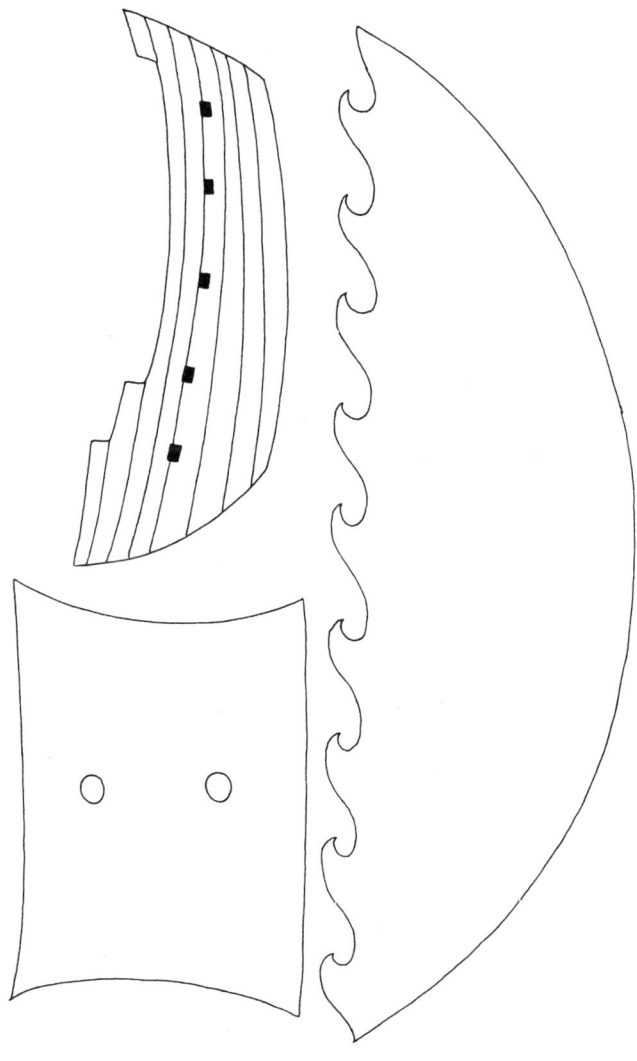

Touch Book (or Box)

On poster board cut into pieces about eight-by-eleven inches, make pictures from materials of different textures. For example, make a footprint out of sandpaper, a shirt or blouse out of a silky fabric, a dog out of fake fur, a window out of slick plastic, a house out of wood (Popsicle sticks), and so on. Use as many different textures as you can.

Have your child close his eyes and feel the picture. Encourage him to use all kinds of descriptive words in telling you about what he feels—words like scratchy, fuzzy, bumpy, slick, and smooth.

Bibliography

Aardema, Verna. *Why Mosquitos Buzz in People's Ears: A West African Tale.* New York: Dial Books for Young Readers, 1975.

Aesop. *Aesop's Fables.* Illustrated by Heidi Holder. New York: Viking Press, 1981.

Aiken, Conrad. *Cats and Bats and Things with Wings.* New York: Atheneum Pubs., 1965.

Alexander, Lloyd. *The High King.* New York: Holt, Rinehart and Winston, 1968.

Aliki. *My Five Senses.* New York: Harper and Row Pubs., 1972.

Allen, Janet. *Exciting Things to Do with Color.* Philadelphia: J. B. Lippincott Co., 1977.

Anno, Mitsumasa. *Anno's Alphabet: An Adventure in Imagination.* New York: Harper and Row Pubs., 1975.

———. *Anno's Counting Book.* New York: Harper and Row Pubs., 1977.

Armstrong, William H. *Sounder.* New York: Harper and Row Pubs., 1969.

Arnstein, Helene S. *Billy and Our New Baby.* New York: Human Sciences Press, 1973.

Balian, Lorna. *Humbug Rabbit.* Nashville: Abingdon Press, 1974.

Barlowe, Dorothea and Sy. *Dinosaurs.* New York: Random House, 1977.

Barth, Edna. *Hearts, Cupids and Red Roses.* Boston: Houghton Mifflin Co., 1971.

———. *Shamrocks, Harps and Shillelaghs.* Boston: Houghton Mifflin Co., 1977.

Besko, Elsa. *Pelle's New Suit.* New York: Harper and Row Pubs., 1929.

Blos, Joan W. *The Gathering of Days.* New York: Charles Scribner's Sons, 1979.

Brown, Marcia. *Once a Mouse . . .* New York: Charles Scribner's Sons, 1961.

———. *Shadow.* New York: Charles Scribner's Sons, 1982.

———. *Stone Soup.* New York: Charles Scribner's Sons, 1947.

Brown, Margaret W. *Goodnight Moon.* New York: Harper and Row Pubs., 1947.

———. *The Little Fireman.* Reading, Massachusetts: Addison-Wesley Publishing Co., 1952.

———. *The Seashore Noisy Book.* New York: Harper and Row Pubs., 1941.

Burton, Virginia Lee. *Mike Mulligan and His Steam Shovel.* Boston: Houghton Mifflin Co., 1977.

Byars, Betsy. *The Summer of the Swans.* New York: Viking Press, 1970.

Carle, Eric. *The Very Hungry Caterpillar.* Cleveland, Ohio: William Collins Pubs., 1969.

Chaucer, Geoffrey. *Chanticleer and the Fox*. New York: Harper and Row Pubs., 1958.

Cole, Joanna. *A Calf is Born*. New York: William Morrow and Co., 1975.

———. *My Puppy is Born*. New York: William Morrow and Co., 1973.

Cole, William. *An Arkful of Animals: Poems for the Very Young*. Boston: Houghton Mifflin Co., 1978.

———. *I Went to the Animal Fair*. Cleveland, Ohio: William Collins Pubs., 1978.

Collier, Ethel. *The Birthday Tree*. New York: Scott Young, 1961.

Cooper, Susan. *The Grey King*. New York: Atheneum Pubs., 1975.

Crews, Donald. *Truck*. New York: Greenwillow Books, 1980.

Cummins, Dorothy. *Favorite Songs for Children*. New York: Putnam Publishing Group, 1965.

Dalgliesh, Alice. *The Fourth of July Story*. New York: Charles Scribner's Sons, 1956.

———. *The Thanksgiving Story*. New York: Charles Scribner's Sons, 1954.

De Paola, Tomie. *Charlie Needs a Cloak*. Englewood Cliffs, New Jersey: Prentice-Hall, 1974.

———. *Strega Nona*. Englewood Cliffs, New Jersey: Prentice-Hall, 1975.

———. *The Clown of God*. New York: Harcourt Brace Jovanovich, 1978.

———. *The Friendly Beasts: An Old English Christmas Carol*. Putnam Publishing Group, 1981.

De Reginers, Beatrice Schenk. *May I Bring a Friend?* New York: Atheneum Pubs., 1964.

De Trevino, Elizabeth Borton. *Juan De Pareja*. New York: Farrar, Straus and Giroux, 1969.

Doane, Pelagie. *A Small Child's Book of Verse*. New York: Oxford University Press, 1948.

Emberley, Barbara. *Drummer Hoff*. Englewood Cliffs, New Jersey: Prentice-Hall, 1967.

Emberley, Ed. *A Birthday Wish*. Boston: Little, Brown and Co., 1977.

———. *Ed Emberley's ABC*. Boston: Little, Brown and Co., 1978.

———. *Green Says Go*. Boston: Little, Brown and Co., 1968.

———. *The Wing on a Flea*. Boston: Little, Brown and Co., 1961.

Ets, Marie Hall. *Gilberto and the Wind*. New York: Viking Press, 1963.

———. *Just Me*. New York: Penguin Books, 1970.

Ets, Marie Hall, and Aurora Labastida. *Nine Days to Christmas*. New York: Viking Press, 1959.

Fox, Paula. *The Slave Dancer*. Scarsdale, New York: Bradbury Press, 1973.

Friskey, Margaret. *Birds We Know*. Chicago: Children's Press, 1981.

Fujikawa, Gyo. *Come Follow Me . . . to the Secret World of Elves and Fairies and Gnomes and Trolls*. New York: Putnam Publishing Group, 1979.

Gag, Wanda. *Millions of Cats*. New York: Putnam Publishing Group, 1980.

Galdone, Paul. *How Many Teeth.* New York: Harper and Row Pubs., 1962.

———. *The Gingerbread Boy.* Boston: Houghton Mifflin Co., 1975.

———. *The Little Red Hen.* Boston: Houghton Mifflin Co., 1973.

George, Jean Craighead. *Julie of the Wolves.* New York: Harper and Row Pubs., 1972.

Glazer, Tom. *Do Your Ears Hang Low?* New York: Doubleday and Co., 1980.

———. *Eye Winker Tom Tinker Chin Chopper.* New York: Doubleday and Co., 1978.

Goble, Paul. *The Girl Who Loved Wild Horses.* Scarsdale, New York: Bradbury Press, 1978.

Grayson, Marion F. *Let's Do Fingerplays.* Bridgeport, Connecticut: Robert B. Luce, 1962.

Greenaway, Kate. *A—Apple Pie.* New York: Frederick Warne and Co., 1886.

Haley, Gail E. *A Story, A Story.* New York: Atheneum Pubs., 1970.

Hall, Donald. *The Oxcart Man.* New York: Viking Press, 1979.

Hamilton, Virginia. *M. C. Higgins, the Great.* New York: Macmillan Publishing Co., 1974.

Hart, Jane, *Singing Bee!* New York: Lothrop, Lee and Shepherd Books, 1982.

Hillman, Priscilla. *A Merry-Mouse Book of Months.* New York: Doubleday and Co., 1980.

Hoban, Russell. *Bedtime for Frances.* New York: Harper and Row Pubs., 1960.

———. *Egg Thoughts and Other Frances Songs.* New York: Harper and Row Pubs., 1972.

Hoban, Tana. *Circles, Triangles and Squares.* New York: Macmillan Publishing Co., 1974.

———. *Count and See.* New York: Macmillan Publishing Co., 1974.

Hogrogian, Nony. *One Fine Day.* New York: Macmillan Publishing Co., 1971.

Hunt, Irene. *Up a Road Slowly.* Cleveland, Ohio: Modern Curriculum Press, 1966.

Janice. *Little Bear's Thanksgiving.* New York: Lothrop, Lee and Shepherd Books, 1967.

Johnson, Hannah Lyons. *From Seed to Jack-o-Lantern.* New York: Lothrop, Lee and Shepherd Books, 1974.

Jordan, Helene J. *Seeds by Wind and Water.* New York: Harper and Row Pubs., 1962.

Keats, Ezra Jack. *The Pet Show.* New York: Macmillan Publishing Co., 1974.

———. *The Snowy Day.* New York: Viking Press, 1962.

Keith, Harold. *Rifles for Watie*. New York: Harper and Row Pubs., 1957.

Kessler, Ethel and Leonard. *Our Tooth Story*. New York: Dodd, Mead and Co., 1972.

Konigsburg, E. L. *From the Mixed-Up Files of Mrs. Basil E. Frankweiler*. New York: Atheneum Pubs., 1967.

Krauss, Ruth. *The Carrot Seed*. New York: Scholastic Book Services, 1971.

Krumgold, Joseph. *Onion John*. New York: Harper and Row Pubs., 1969.

Kunhardt, Dorothy. *Pat the Bunny*. Racine, Wisconsin: Western Publishing Co., 1962.

Lambert, David, and L. B. Halstead. *Dinosaurs*. New York: Watts, Franklin, Inc., 1982.

Langstaff, John. *Frog Went A-Courtin'*. New York: Harcourt Brace Jovanovich, 1955.

Lasly, Marion. *Picture Book of Musical Instruments*. New York: Lothrop, Lee and Shepherd Books, 1942.

Latham, Jean L. *Carry On, Mr. Bowditch*. Boston: Houghton Mifflin Co., 1955.

Leodhas, Sorche Nic. *Always Room for One More*. New York: Holt, Rinehart and Winston, 1965.

L'Engle, Madeleine. *A Wrinkle in Time*. New York: Farrar, Straus and Giroux, 1962.

Lenski, Lois. *I Went for a Walk*. Henry Z. Walck, 1958.

———. *On a Summer Day*. Henry Z. Walck, 1953.

———. *Policeman Small*. Henry Z. Walck, 1962.

———. *Spring Is Here*. Henry Z. Walck, 1945.

Lewellyn, John. *Moon, Sun and Stars*. Chicago: Children's Press, 1981.

Lionni, Leo. *Little Blue and Little Yellow*. New York: Astor-Honor, 1959.

Lobel, Arnold. *A Tree Full of Pigs*. New York: Greenwillow Books, 1979.

———. *Fables*. New York: Harper and Row Pubs., 1980.

———. *Frog and Toad Together*. New York: Harper and Row Pubs., 1980.

The Lord is My Shepherd: The Twenty Fourth Psalm. Illustrated by Tasha Tudor. New York: Putnam Publishing Group, 1980.

McCloskey, Robert. *Make Way for Ducklings*. New York: Viking Press, 1969.

———. *Time of Wonder*. New York: Viking Press, 1957.

McCord, Anne. *The Scholastic Fun Fact Book of Dinosaurs*. New York: Scholastic Book Services, 1977.

McCord, David. *Every Time I Climb a Tree*. Boston: Little, Brown and Co., 1967.

McDermott, Gerald. *Arrow to the Sun: A Pueblo Indian Tale*. New York: Viking Press, 1974.

McFarland, Willma. *For a Child*. Philadelphia: Westminster Press, 1947.

McPhail, David. *The Train*. New York: Penguin Books, 1979.

Mayer, Mercer. *A Boy, A Dog and A Frog.* New York: Dial Books for Young Readers, 1967.

―――. *Professor Wormbog in Search for the Zipperump-a-Zoo.* Racine, Wisconsin: Western Publishing Co., 1976.

Miner, O. Irene. *Plants We Know.* Chicago: Children's Press, 1981.

Mosel, Arlene. *The Funny Little Woman.* New York: E. P. Dutton, 1972.

Musgrove, Margaret W. *Ashanti to Zulu: African Traditions.* New York: Dial Books for Young Readers, 1976.

Nash, Ogden. *The Moon is Shining Bright.* New York: Harper and Row Pubs., 1953.

―――. *The New Nutcracker Suite and Other Innocent Verses.* Boston: Little, Brown and Co., 1961.

Ness, Evaline. *Sam, Bangs and Moonshine.* New York: Holt, Rinehart and Winston, 1966.

Neville, Emily. *It's Like This, Cat.* New York: Harper and Row Pubs., 1963.

O'Brien, Robert C. *Mrs. Frisby and the Rats of NIMH.* New York: Atheneum Pubs., 1971.

O'Dell, Scott. *Island of the Blue Dolphins.* Boston: Houghton Mifflin Co., 1960.

Parish, Peggy. *Amelia Bedelia.* New York: Scholastic Book Services, 1970.

―――. *Dinosaur Time.* New York: Harper and Row Pubs., 1974.

Patterson, Katherine. *Bridge to Terabithia.* New York: Harper and Row Pubs., 1977.

―――. *Jacob Have I Loved.* New York: Harper and Row Pubs., 1980.

Paul, Aileen. *Kid's Gardening.* New York: Doubleday and Co., 1972.

Peterson, David. *Airplanes.* Chicago: Children's Press, 1981.

―――. *Airports.* Chicago: Children's Press, 1981.

Peterson, Isabel J. *The First Book of Poetry.* New York: Franklin Watts, 1954.

Piper, Watty. *The Little Engine That Could.* New York: Scholastic Book Services, 1979.

Potter, Beatrix. *The Tale of Peter Rabbit.* Illustrated by Allen Atkinson. New York: Alfred A. Knopf, 1982.

Podendorf, Illa. *Baby Animals.* Chicago: Children's Press, 1981.

―――. *Pets.* Chicago: Children's Press, 1954.

―――. *Sounds We Hear.* Hale, 1955.

―――. *The True Book of Seasons.* Chicago: Children's Press, 1955.

Ransome, Arthur. *The Fool of the World and the Flying Ship.* New York: Farrar, Straus and Giroux, 1968.

Raskin, Ellen. *Westing Game.* New York: E. P. Dutton, 1978.

Reiss, John J. *Colors.* Scarsdale, New York: Bradbury Press, 1969.

―――. *Shapes.* Scarsdale, New York: Bradbury Press, 1974.

Richardson, Frederick. *Mother Goose.* Chicago: Rand McNally and Co., 1979.

Robbins, Ruth. *Baboushka and the Three Kings*. Orleans, Massachusetts: Parnassus Press, 1960.

Rockwell, Harlow. *My Doctor*. New York: Macmillan Publishing Co., 1973.

Selsam, Millicent E. *Egg to Chick*. New York: Harper and Row Pubs., 1970.

————. *Is This a Baby Dinosaur?* New York: Harper and Row Pubs., 1972.

————. *Sea Monsters of Long Ago*. New York: Scholastic Book Services, 1978.

Selsam, Millicent E., and Jerome Wexler. *Eat the Fruit, Plant the Seed*. New York: William Morrow and Co., 1980.

Sendak, Maurice. *Where the Wild Things Are*. New York: Harper and Row Pubs., 1963.

Seuss, Dr. *Green Eggs and Ham*. New York: Random House, 1960.

————. *If I Ran the Zoo*. New York: Random House, 1980.

Silverstein, Alvin. *Itch, Sniffle and Sneeze*. New York: Scholastic Book Services, 1978.

Sislowitz, Marcel. *Look! How Your Eyes Can See*. New York: Coward, McCann and Geoghegan Inc., 1977.

Skaar, Grace. *The Very Little Dog*. Reading, Massachusetts: Addison-Wesley Publishing Co., 1947.

Slobodkin, Louis. *Trick or Treat*. New York: Macmillan Publishing Co., 1967.

Slobodkina, Esphyr. *Caps for Sale*. Reading, Massachusetts: Addison-Wesley Publishing Co., 1947.

Smith, Doris Susan. *The Travels of J. B. Rabbit*. New York: Putnam Publishing Group, 1982.

Sorensen, Virginia. *Miracles on Maple Hill*. New York: Harcourt Brace Jovanovich, 1956.

Speare, Elizabeth G. *The Bronze Bow*. Boston: Houghton Mifflin Co., 1961.

————. *The Witch of Blackbird Pond*. Boston: Houghton Mifflin Co., 1958.

Spier, Peter. *Christmas*. New York: Doubleday and Co., 1982.

————. *Noah's Ark*. New York: Doubleday and Co., 1977.

————. *Rain*. New York: Doubleday and Co., 1982.

Steig, William. *Sylvester and the Magic Pebble*. New York: Simon and Schuster, 1969.

Stevenson, James. *That Terrible Halloween Night*. New York: Greenwillow Books, 1980.

Stevenson, Robert Louis. *A Child's Garden of Verse*. New York: Random House, 1978.

Taylor, Mildred. *Roll of Thunder, Hear My Cry*. New York: Dial Books for Young Readers, 1976.

Trealease, Jim. *The Read Aloud Handbook*. New York: Penguin Books, 1982.

Tresselt, Alvin. *Follow the Wind*. New York: Lothrop, Lee and Shepherd Books, 1950.

————. *Johnny Maple-Leaf.* New York: Lothrop, Lee and Shepherd Books, 1948.

————. *The Mitten.* New York: Lothrop, Lee and Shepherd Books, 1964.

————. *White Snow, Bright Snow.* New York: Lothrop, Lee and Shepherd Books, 1947.

Udry, Janice M. *A Tree Is Nice.* New York: Harper and Row Pubs., 1956.

Waber, Bernard. *Lyle, Lyle Crocodile.* Boston: Houghton Mifflin Co., 1965.

Walker, M. *Wild Animals That Help People.* New York: David McKay Co., 1977.

Ward, Lynd. *The Biggest Bear.* Boston: Houghton Mifflin Co., 1973.

Watson, Clyde. *Father Fox's Pennyrhymes.* New York: Scholastic Book Services, 1975.

Watson, Jane Werner. *My Friend the Dentist.* Racine, Wisconsin: Western Publishing Co., 1972.

Wells, Rosemary. *Morris' Disappearing Bag.* New York: Dial Books for Young Readers, 1978.

Willard, Nancy. *A Visit to William Blake's Inn.* New York: Harcourt Brace Jovanovich, 1981.

Winn, Marie. *What Shall We Do and Allee Galloo!* New York: Harper and Row Pubs., 1963.

Wojciechowska, Maia. *Shadow of a Bull.* New York: Atheneum Pubs., 1964.

Wyler, Rose, and Gerald Ames. *Prove It.* New York: Harper and Row Pubs., 1963.

Van Allsburg, Chris. *Jumanji.* Boston: Houghton Mifflin Co., 1981.

Van Woerkom, Dorothy. *Alexandra the Rock-Eater.* New York: Alfred A. Knopf, 1978.

Voight, Cynthia. *Dicey's Song.* New York: Atheneum Pubs., 1982.

Viorst, Judith. *Alexander and the Terrible, Horrible, No Good, Very Bad Day.* New York: Atheneum Pubs., 1976.

Yashima, Taro. *Crow Boy.* New York: Viking Press, 1955.

Zemach, Harvey. *Duffy and the Devil.* New York: Farrar, Straus and Giroux, 1973.

————. *The Judge.* New York: Farrar, Straus and Giroux, 1969.

Index